HOMEMADE SOURDOUGH

A Quintet Book

Published in 2015 by Voyageur Press, an imprint of Quarto Publishing Group USA Inc., 400 First Avenue North, Suite 400, Minneapolis, MN 55401 USA

Voyageur Press titles are also available at discounts in bulk quantity for industrial or sales-promotional use. For details write to Special Sales Manager at Quarto Publishing Group USA Inc., 400 First Avenue North, Suite 400, Minneapolis, MN 55401 USA.

To find out more about our books, visit us online at www.voyageurpress.com.

ISBN: 978-0-7603-4734-8

QTT:PSOU

This book was conceived, designed, and produced by:
Quintet Publishing Limited
4th Floor, Sheridan House
114–116 Western Road
Hove, East Sussex BN3 1DD
United Kingdom

Project Editor: Cara Frost-Sharratt
Designer: Tania Gomes
Photographer: Jon Whitaker
Food Stylist: Lucy Heeley
Art Director: Michael Charles
Editorial Director: Emma Bastow
Publisher: Mark Searle

Printed and bound in China By RR Donnelley

10 9 8 7 6 5 4 3 2 1

HOMEMADE SOURDOUGH

MASTERING THE ART AND SCIENCE OF
BAKING WITH STARTERS AND WILD YEAST

JANE MASON
RECIPES BY ED WOOD ET AL.

Voyageur
Press

CONTENTS

FOREWORD

This is my third book about bread and I am delighted that it is a book on sourdough baking. I started experimenting with sourdough a long time ago when a friend gave me some of her wheat sourdough starter and a photocopy of an old American sourdough book that I still treasure. That wheat starter is now the stuff of legends, having been born in 1857, lived in many different countries, survived bus journeys and transatlantic flights, and lived through an accidental five-year exile to the back of the fridge. It is living proof of the hardiness of a sourdough culture.

Years later I bought some backferment from a health food store in Germany and started experimenting with that, and then I got into baking with a rye starter. Along the way I have experimented with spelt, buckwheat, and sprouted grain starters. Baking with sourdough is a life-long journey and every day is exciting, with a little frisson of danger! I would love to be able to tell you that every loaf has been a beauty but that would be a lie. There have been some spectacularly ugly loaves along the way but—repeat the mantra after me—everything is good toasted, even if it's ugly.

In this book we have included recipes for just two starters—rye and wheat—as you can achieve a great deal in the world of sourdough baking with just these two. It keeps things simple and you won't have numerous jars of starters cluttering up your refrigerator. If you like, you can make four starters because the process for making and using a light rye and a dark rye starter are the same, and the process for making a whole wheat starter and a white wheat starter are the same. This flexibility enables you to bake whole rye or whole wheat bread, or light rye or white wheat bread as your tastes dictate. If you get hooked (and beware, you may) you can go on experimenting forever with different grains, starters, and doughs. There really is no end to what you can do.

Finally, it's worth mentioning that while baking sourdough bread might seem daunting—people frequently say that it takes forever—the reality is that it is actually simpler than baking other types of bread. That's because sourdough does its thing over so many hours that you're free to leave it and go to work or go to bed. Of course, all the recipes differ but there are plenty that will work around you and your schedule. The actual time you need to spend interacting with your dough is a matter of minutes, and once you make your starter you can keep it for life!

Jane Mason

INTRODUCTION

Over the past few years, sourdough baking has enjoyed a resurgence, as people discover that they actually like chewing their bread and enjoy the stronger flavor that sourdough offers. In addition, many people find they can eat and enjoy sourdough bread without feeling bloated and uncomfortable the way they sometimes do when they eat "regular" bread.

BAKE YOUR OWN

Buying sourdough at a supermarket or market where you can't talk to the baker can be a bit of a risky business: there are no clear labeling laws for bread, and the dough of many "sourdough" loaves is actually made with regular yeast with the addition of sourdough powders for flavor. That's where this book comes in—here you will find all the information you need, and a collection of recipes that are simple and clear, so you can have a go at making your own sourdough bread.

DEMYSTIFYING SOURDOUGH

Sourdough baking seems to have acquired a mystique, and one of the aims of this book is to demystify it. The truth is that baking sourdough bread is simple and intuitive—anyone can do it. One of the reasons sourdough baking seems so complicated is that there are many different words used in the world of sourdough baking—some mean the same thing and some don't—and different bakers use the same word to mean different things. Starter, poolish, biga, sponge, pre-dough, batter: the terms are often interchangeable and it can get a bit confusing. Don't worry, read on and we'll list the terms that are used throughout the book, and define them for you.

Another reason baking sourdough bread seems complicated is that there are about a million ways to bake it. Again, don't worry—there is no one right way. Some bakers may go through stages that others do not, and some bread requires a particular process while other bread requires something quite different. The truth is that it all depends on what you are baking and how you choose to bake it.

This book aims to demystify the process of baking sourdough bread and to set out a simple, consistent process that will result in delicious and beautiful loaves time and time again. Of course, there are plenty of other books and many other ways to bake sourdough bread, and we encourage you to experiment and find the ways that work for you. We hope that this book helps you on your journey.

BREAD BASICS

IT'S ALL IN THE RISE

In order for bread to rise you need air bubbles to form in the dough, and you need the dough to have the strength to maintain those air bubbles and expand. So, the first thing you need is flour that will develop into dough that will puff out as the air bubbles form, rather than expand a bit and collapse.

Think of bubble gum. You can blow big bubbles with bubble gum because it was created especially to blow bubbles. However, "regular" chewing gum only enables you to blow small bubbles before they pop. It is the same with flour: some grains make flour that creates a dough that is like bubble gum so, when air is inserted into it, it can support the formation of big bubbles. Other grains make flour that creates a dough that is like "regular" chewing gum so, when air is inserted into it, it will only support the development of small bubbles before they collapse.

ADDING YEAST

The bubbles in bread are created when the yeast that is added to dough starts to eat the sugars in the flour, drink the water and burp. Seriously, when yeast begins to eat and drink, it emits carbon dioxide gas just like us. You can prepare your dough with yeast from a packet or with a sourdough starter, which is simply a paste of flour and water in which natural yeast has been trapped. Yeast is a micro-organism that lives in the air. There are yeasts in the air all around us, and making a sourdough starter is a way of bottling them.

CHOOSING YOUR LOAF

The first thing to decide before you start baking is what kind of bread you would like, how you are going to use it, and how much interaction you want with the dough as you prepare it for baking. These are important considerations because bread really does have a function and, like anything, there is a trade-off between time and effort, and results.

If you like the closed, dense structure of northern European-style bread—which you slice thinly and top with smoked fish, strong cheese, or butter and jam—you may want to use a rye sourdough starter and bake bread with a high rye content. The benefit of this is that you will typically prepare the dough and put it straight into a tin to rise before baking, so it requires almost no work at all. However, if you prefer French- or Italian-style bread, with a more open, fluffy crumb that you tear to dip into sauce, or use to make sandwiches that the crust keeps together, you may want to use a wheat starter and bake with a high wheat content. To do this you will need to prepare your dough in two or three stages. Many people like their bread with big holes. To achieve this, you need:

1. Wet dough that blisters easily as the bubbles are formed.
2. High protein flour to support the development of big bubbles.
3. Lots of stretching and folding to elongate the bubbles, thin the dough membranes, and give the yeast fresh air and food.
4. A very hot oven and baking stone or tray, which results in a very crispy crust due to rapid baking.

Extra proof for extra flavor

Many of the recipes in this book call for you to mix up the final dough, knead if required, shape it immediately and, when properly fermented, bake. However, if you would like to build the flavor of your dough and break down the flour more with a longer fermentation, you can do it.

Dough with a high rye content requires little or no kneading, but low or no rye-content dough—such as the recipes in Everyday Wheat, Flavored Wheat, and Sweet Bread—benefit from kneading to activate the gluten and ensure a nice rise. If you would like to ferment the dough for longer than the recipes call for, you can do one of the following:

1. Mix all the ingredients together, cover the bowl, and leave it for 2 to 3 hours before kneading. The flour will begin to ferment and the gluten is activated: this is called "autolysing." You could also put the bowl in the refrigerator overnight. Then, simply knead and shape the dough, following the recipe instructions for proofing and baking.

2. You can knead the ingredients and pop them back in the bowl. Cover and leave the dough for 2 to 3 hours (or overnight in the refrigerator, if you like) then de-gas and shape the dough. Follow the recipe instructions for proofing and baking.

If you have put the dough in the refrigerator, it will be cold, and will take several hours to come to room temperature and rise. You shouldn't leave your dough for much longer than outlined above. If your dough is too fermented it simply won't have any structure left to rise properly, and you will be left with very heavy loaves that may not brown nicely in the oven.

THE VERSATILE LOAF

The point is that there are many types of bread and many different styles of baking. For everyday bread, you may want something simple with only one or two steps, so you can get on with your life. But from time to time you may have the inclination to stay at home and fiddle with your dough at regular intervals to achieve a very different result. The important thing is to do what works for you.

Whether round or square, open or closed, baked in a tin or free form, made using rye or wheat (or anything else) the main shared features of bread made with a sourdough starter—rather than packaged yeast—are the slightly acidic smell and taste, and the distinctive chewy texture. These characteristics are not for everyone—some people love them and some people don't.

SOURDOUGH BASICS

The process of baking with sourdough is similar to that for baking with fresh or dried yeast. There are, however, a few important differences:

1. It is very easy to make your own sourdough starter, but if you don't have a lab you can't make your own yeast—unless you already have some.

2. Sourdough starters can be stored indefinitely, as long as they are stored properly, whereas commercial yeast has a shelf life (unless you store it in the freezer).

3. The amount of sourdough starter you need to make bread is different to the amount of fresh or dried yeast you need to make bread. The amount of starter also depends on the base flour of the starter, the type of flour used to refresh the starter, and the type of flour you use to make the final dough. Until you are familiar with your starters and how they behave when you refresh and bake with them, you can use recipes—that's what this book is for!

4. The sourdough starter must be refreshed (airy or bubbly, and sweet smelling) to make bread that rises. You can either feed flour and water to your starter every day to keep it constantly refreshed (ideal if you are baking in large quantities every day) or allow it to go dormant between bakes. To do this, simply leave it in the refrigerator (in an airtight container) or freezer, or dry it out until the day before you are ready to bake. At that point, refresh it by mixing some of the starter with some flour and water, according to the recipe. It takes between 4 and 24 hours to refresh a dormant sourdough starter, depending on how long it has been sleeping. You will know the starter is refreshed when it is lively, bubbly, and sweet smelling.

5. Sourdough bread takes longer to rise. You can make good bread at home with commercial yeast in about 4 hours (minimum and on a hot day) but sourdough bread can take much longer. Don't panic, as most of that time is spent with the dough sitting around contemplating itself, and it does not require your attention.

6. It is this enforced longer fermentation (the time the dough is sitting around in its various stages before you bake it) that makes sourdough bread easier to digest than bread made in a shorter time. Over the hours, the yeast is actually eating the flour and breaking it down so we can digest it efficiently and quickly extract the nutrients. This means that it doesn't hang around fermenting in our digestive system, making us feel bloated.

Storing your sourdough starter

- Put it in an airtight container and freeze it (defrost before you use it).
- Weigh it and smear it on greaseproof paper, then let it dry completely. Weigh it again, crumble it and pop it in an airtight container. Store on a shelf in a cupboard and write the difference between the "wet weight" and "dry weight" on the container. That is the amount of water you need to add to reconstitute it before you use it.
- Put it in an airtight container and store in the refrigerator.
- The starter will always come back to life when you refresh it according to the recipe instructions.

7. Sourdough bread doesn't rise as much as bread made with commercial yeast (which is more powerful). With commercial yeast the dough should at least double in size at whatever stage, whereas sourdough bread will only rise by about one-and-a-half times before the yeast begins to lose its puff. The relative weakness of the natural yeast in a sourdough starter is one reason why the dough should be wetter than you may be used to. All else being equal, wetter dough expands more easily than dryer dough.

The dough is ready to bake when it passes the probe test. Poke the loaf gently with your finger, making a little indentation. If the dough springs back and the indentation disappears in under a minute, it is ready to bake. If the dough is firm and the indentation stays, it is not ready. If you put the dough in the oven at this stage, it may crack because the dough is not sufficiently relaxed to withstand the "oven spring" without cracking. It will be a little dense but it will still taste good. On the other hand, if the dough is very soft and airy you have let it over rise. In this instance, give it a little more flour and another knead, shape it again and let it rise again. Chalk it up to experience and have fun trying again.

8. Sourdough bread may taste a little stronger and have a chewier texture than bread made with commercial yeast. Sourdough bread doesn't need to taste sour: the longer you take to put your final dough together, the more acidic it will smell and taste. If you like a more acidic taste, select the recipes that take a lot of time to make. If you prefer a less acidic taste, choose recipes that take less time. As you develop your baking skills you will be able to adjust any recipe to suit your tastes. The term "sourdough" is therefore a little misleading, and many bakers refer to sourdough bread as wild yeast bread or natural yeast bread instead.

MAKING YOUR OWN STARTERS

It is simple to make your own starters and there are many ways to do it. Some recipes ask you to use a little yeast, and some ask for a little grape, apple, vinegar, or pineapple. I have even heard of one that asks for beer. Some recipes ask you to throw away some of your starter every day while you are making it. You can experiment to your heart's content or you can follow the recipes in this book. All you need are flour and water.

In the book we use two different starters: rye (see page 40 for rye starter recipe) and wheat (see page 71 for wheat starter recipe). They behave differently and you may as well make one of each so you can bake your way through the book and decide which one you like better or whether you like both. You can make starters out of many other grains (any other grain, if I am being honest) but we only have space for two.

BASIC TERMS

A shared vocabulary is always a good thing so that everyone understands everyone else. Below are the terms that you will find used throughout the book. When you read them, you know exactly what we are referring to.

Sourdough starter

For the purposes of this book, the sourdough starter is the smelly gloop in the refrigerator that you need to wake up (or refresh) before you put your dough together. Don't worry if your sourdough starter is really smelly, and don't worry if it has separated so there is liquid floating on the top of a mass of sediment—that's normal. It's called hooch, and you can ferment other things with this (like cabbage to make sauerkraut or fruit to make alcohol, but that's a whole other book). There's also no need to worry if the liquid is a dark brown color. The time to start worrying is if your starter is moldy, and if this is the case, throw it away. As long as you store your starter correctly (in an airtight container in the refrigerator, in the freezer, or dehydrated) it will be just fine.

Refreshed starter

For the purposes of this book, refreshed starter is the sweet-smelling result of adding flour and water to the possibly smelly sourdough starter from the refrigerator. How you refresh your starter varies according to the type of starter you are refreshing, and the type of bread you are making. Don't worry, the instructions are in every single recipe.

Pre-dough (not always necessary)

When there is an intermediate step (or steps) between refreshing the sourdough starter and kneading and shaping the final dough, this mixing together of ingredients is called making a pre-dough. Not all recipes call for a pre-dough.

Final dough

The final mixture that is eventually shaped and baked.

Your first sourdough bread

- Start by preparing a starter following the method on page 40 for a rye starter, and on page 71 for a wheat starter.
- Take a look at the equipment list on pages 18–20.
- Read through the advice on pages 26–27 on Storing and Using a Sourdough Starter.
- If you are new to baking with sourdough, you may like to begin by making the Basic Sourdough Batter Bread on page 25. This quick bread is a great way to build your confidence before moving onto some of the more complex recipes later in the book.
- Once you have mastered the basic recipes, have a go at some different techniques—try Pita Bread on pages 50–51 and Raisin Rye on 62–65.

INGREDIENTS

YEAST

Commercial yeast that we can see and hold in our hands was invented in the 1850s but was not widely used until after the Second World War. However, we have been baking leavened bread for an incredible 10,000 years. Yes, sourdough bread has been around for a long time.

We have already talked about the fact that the yeast we add to sourdough bread does not come from a packet: we can't see it or hold it. The yeast we add to sourdough bread is, in fact, trapped in the paste of flour and water that we call the sourdough starter. So, the starter contains the yeast.

Because you need to account for the weight of the flour and water that make the paste in which the yeast is trapped, you need relatively more starter than yeast from a packet to make the same amount of bread. Also, because you are adding starter (with the consistency of sticky paste) rather than yeast (with the consistency of a powder or crumbly paste) to flour and water to make the dough, your sourdough bread dough will always be sticky.

FLOUR

From field to field, season to season, mill to mill, and bag to bag, flour changes. It absorbs more or less water, is more or less stretchy, has more or less flavor, and has different color variations. Bakers need to adjust to those changes, for example, by adding more or less water to the dough, letting the dough rise for more or less time, or expecting a higher or a lower rise.

Time and experience will teach you how to adjust, and you will constantly be adjusting as the seasons turn, as you change the brand (or even bag) of flour you use, and as the conditions in the kitchen change. No bread recipe is a science and you will learn which

texture of dough leads you to bake the bread you love. Never give up—your loaves may not be beauties all the time (I still get some ugly ducklings) but as we've already learnt, everything is good toasted.

I recommend you use stone-ground flour if you can get it. I believe it is more nutritious because it is processed in a gentler way than flour that is aggressively processed by metal rollers—that heat the flour as they mill it—and then hydraulically pressed through extraordinarily fine screens. However, stone-ground flour is not always readily available and it is more expensive.

Wheat flour

Wheat flour is easily available in most countries around the world. It is available in different strengths and levels of fineness and whiteness. Unfortunately, there is no universal system for labeling flour so, if you move around, you may need to ask professional bakers what the names or numbers on the bag of flour mean. Most recipes in this book call for "bread" flour. You may see it labeled as "high-protein flour," "extra strong flour," or "strong flour." You may also see it labeled as "durum flour". If you can't find strong flour, use what you can get. Bread baked with "soft" flour (plain or all-purpose flour) gives different results—the loaf may be smaller, it may rise more quickly, and the bread will be softer in the mouth—but it will still be delicious.

Einkorn, emmer, spelt, and kamut flour

All these flours are milled from grains that are distant cousins of wheat. They all have stretchy gluten and perform in a similar way to wheat flour. However, depending on how and where they are grown, they may be more or less strong and stretchy, or more or less absorbent than the wheat flour you are used to.

You can use these flours as substitutes for wheat flour, but every time you change grain you will notice a change in the amount of liquid the flour will absorb (you can modify the recipe by adding more or less liquid). The texture of the dough will also change (it may be more or less stretchy and expand more or less than when using wheat flour) and, of course, the appearance, texture and flavor of the final bread will be different. Again, time and experience will help you make those changes with ease, confidence, and style.

Rye flour

Rye has gluten but it is not stretchy like the gluten in the wheat family, so it doesn't handle or perform in the same way. You can't substitute wheat for rye or rye for wheat. Also, rye is much more absorbent than wheat so expect it to absorb a lot more liquid. Your rye dough should always be wet—anything less than wet leads to the leaden loaves that people understandably don't appreciate very much. If you bake one of these, put it down to experience. Add more liquid next time and, in the meantime, slice your leaden rye very, very thinly and toast it. Remember the mantra? That's right—everything is good toasted.

Non-glutinous flour

There are more non-glutinous grains than glutinous grains. Millet, barley, rice, quinoa, and buckwheat are all examples of non-glutinous grains that are milled into flour. They are not substitutes for grains with gluten—they can make lovely bread but you need to treat them in a specialized way to do so.

Sprouted flour

Sprouted flour is becoming very popular and it's fun to work with. In general, you can substitute sprouted flour for non-sprouted flour. However, the dough will feel and perform differently and the final bread will look very different too. When you buy sprouted

grains, there are usually instructions on the packet to advise you how to use it and what to expect.

WATER

Use water straight from your cold tap, or filtered water at room temperature. Sourdough bread does not need warm water, and the only thing that will kill yeast is heat. So don't second-guess or stress about your water temperature—just use regular water.

SALT

Bread needs salt for flavor so please use it. Salt slows down yeast activity, so you add it partway through the kneading process. If you find you forget to add the salt when you're kneading, add it at the beginning; it won't make much difference to the final product.

EQUIPMENT

MASON JAR OR CLIPPED TUPPERWARE

Store your starter in a mason jar or a plastic container with clip-down sides. A jam jar is risky, as your starter will continue to ferment and thus let off carbon dioxide gas as it goes to sleep in your refrigerator. Jam jars don't have a mechanism for allowing gas to leave them and there's a possibility that the jar will shatter. Mason jars, on the other hand, let air out without letting air in, and plastic containers are fine as long as they are properly airtight and all sides snap down. Plastic containers that just have a snap-on lid are not sufficiently airtight and you risk killing your starter by using them.

BAKING PANS

Baking pans are great for many reasons:
- You can clearly see how the dough is moving —has it risen and by how much?
- Your loaves will look perfect every time with no unseemly bulges that accompany a poorly shaped loaf that you have proofed in a basket.
- When you grease a pan properly (with hard fat like butter or lard) the bread will come out of the pan every time. With baskets there is always a little uncertainly—will it or won't it stick?

PROOFING BASKETS (BANNETON)

Proofing baskets (see photograph above) are made of cane or pressed fibers, and they hold the dough during its final rise. We learnt to work with cane long before we learnt to work with metal so they have been used to shape bread for hundreds, if not thousands, of years. Proofing baskets give the baked loaf an attractive finish (with rings of flour on top of the loaves). You can buy them from cooking or baking stores, and from specialist websites.

Before using the proofing basket, season it by painting a thin mixture of cornstarch and water all over the basket with a small paintbrush and leave it to dry. When proofing sourdough loaves in proofing baskets, liberally flour both the basket and the dough to make sure it doesn't stick. Place the shaped dough in the basket upside down. This is because you turn the dough out of the basket and onto a baking sheet to bake it—you don't put proofing baskets in the oven. After a few uses, scrub the basket with hot, soapy water and let it dry completely before you use it again. They do need washing from time to time or tiny bugs may take up residence.

Today, you can buy proofing baskets made of plastic as well as cane. They work well, the bread looks authentic, and they can go in the dishwasher.

OTHER CONTAINERS

Ceramic or glass bowls, strainers, flower pots, saucepans, frying pans…I have probably tried them all, given that I have been in plenty of places which have neither tins nor proofing baskets. If the container is ovenproof and you want to bake your bread in it, make sure you grease it well with a hard fat before putting the dough inside. If the container isn't ovenproof, line it with a tea towel that you have floured liberally before gently laying your shaped, floured dough in it. As with shaping in a proofing basket, place your shaped dough in the container upside down, as you will turn it out of the container onto a baking sheet to bake it.

LINEN OR COTTON CLOTHS

Baking is very tea towel intensive. No matter how many you have, you always seem to need more. Certain types of bread (notably baguettes and ciabattas) are proofed on cloths, and heavy linen cloths made specifically for proofing are now readily available from baking stores or dedicated websites. Flour the cloth and the dough well to ensure it doesn't stick and put the dough on upside down to proof. When the dough is ready, pick it up, turn it over and lay it on the baking sheet. You don't have to do this, but it gives the bread a nice, floury look.

BAKING SHEETS

If you proof your bread in, or on, anything other than a pan you will need some good baking sheets. It is worth paying a little extra for sturdy sheets that do not warp in the oven. Even if your sheet states it is non-stick, it pays to line the sheet when you bake bread—you can use polenta, semolina, or non-stick parchment paper. If using polenta or semolina, simply scatter some liberally on the sheet and place the dough on top—they act as a barrier between the dough and the sheet. If you're using parchment paper make sure it is clearly labeled as non-stick. Tear a piece from the roll, fold or cut it to fit your sheet, and place the dough directly on the paper. You can reuse parchment paper until it falls apart.

LAME

A lame is a straight-edged razor on a stick that bakers use to make the cuts in their loaves. A thin, sharp blade handled with confidence and panache will make a beautiful pattern on your crust and help control any cracking that may occur as your loaves are baking. There are dozens of videos on the internet about how to use a lame to best advantage, but be warned—it's not as easy as it looks. Your first few attempts will leave you with what look like healed scars on your bread, but persevere, as it will get easier and your cuts will get better. Lames are readily available on specialist baking websites.

BOWLS

You will need some big bowls to refresh the sourdough starter and to build your dough. It's a good idea to have a few in the cupboard for when you want to make more than one loaf.

PLASTIC SCRAPERS

Plastic scrapers will change your life. Sourdough dough is sticky, and scrapers help you knead, shape, cut, and move the dough around without leaving half of it either on your hands or on the surface. They also help you clean up more easily by enabling you to scrape down your counter.

PLASTIC SHOWER CAPS

Sourdough bread takes time to rise, so covering the dough with a tea towel can result in the dough drying out. Also, as the dough is sticky, a tea towel may pull the top surface of the dough off as you pull the towel away from the dough. Shower caps, on the other hand, are pretty airtight because they are elasticated, and because they are puckered and pleated, you can fit them around the edge of a tin or bowl and puff them up to give the dough plenty of headroom to rise without sticking to anything. You don't need anything fancy—you can use the kind that you find in hotels—and you can buy them in bulk (they're not expensive) from hotel supply companies or from Amazon or other online stores.

DIGITAL SCALES AND MEASURING CUPS AND SPOONS

Although sourdough baking is not a precise science, there are some ratios you need to respect in order to get good results. The ratio between the amounts of sourdough starter to water to flour is one that's important, and the ratio between refreshed starter to water to flour is another. Beginners should measure as accurately as possible, but with just a little experience you can bake by feeling.

BAKING STONE

In some countries bread is baked by sliding the dough directly onto the floor of the oven, and you can mimic this environment by buying a baking stone and popping the dough straight on that to bake. If you want to use this method, you will also need to buy a peel. This is a long-handled instrument with a "paddle" on the end—you may have seen them used in pizza restaurants. Stones and peels are expensive but many people use them at home and swear by them, so it could be a good investment.

A cheaper alternative is to buy a couple of very good-quality metal baking sheets. Place the metal sheets in the oven to heat while the oven is heating. When you are ready to bake, remove the sheet and line it with non-stick paper immediately (remember it's hot) or sprinkle with a layer of polenta or semolina. Place the dough on top and then pop the sheet straight back in the oven.

OVEN

Sourdough bread really likes heat, and the higher your oven can go, the better the result will be. Investing in a new oven is expensive, but investing in an oven thermometer to test if your oven reaches the correct temperature is not. If your oven is way out, get an engineer to calibrate it. A good-quality electric oven is the best oven for bread, as they can reach a high temperature and the heat is evenly distributed. Gas ovens tend to have uneven heat distribution, and fan ovens that consistently circulate hot air around the oven can dry out the surface of the bread.

MIXER

Stand mixers help when kneading but I recommend you begin kneading by hand to become accustomed to the texture of the dough. If you don't touch the dough you can't test the texture or compare textures between one recipe and another, and one grain and another. There is no "right" texture—different recipes will have different textures and it's important to learn that. Once you get to know the texture you want to achieve, you can knead in a machine and test for texture by giving the dough a little squeeze to see if it is soft or wet enough. Knowing how different textures of dough perform is a matter of experience, and over time you will become more confident and be able to adjust mid-knead in order to achieve the desired results.

PLANT MISTER

A good, old-fashioned plant mister is very useful for misting the top of a loaf in order to "stick" ingredients like seeds onto it. It can also be useful for spaying the inside of the oven to increase humidity for certain bakes. There is mixed opinion on whether it is useful to spray inside the oven but if you want to experiment, the plant mister works very well.

Equipment essentials
If you are new to breadmaking or simply don't fancy forking out on specialist equipment, the following list will enable you to get started:
- Mason jar or clipped tupperware
- Baking pans in your chosen sizes
- Baking sheet
- Bowls
- Scales
- Measuring spoons
- Measuring cups
- Oven thermometer (particularly if you have a gas oven)

BATTER BREAD

For anyone new to sourdough, batter breads are the perfect place to start. The Basic Sourdough Batter Bread on page 25 really couldn't be easier and will give you the confidence to move onto some of the more complex recipes later in the book.

BATTER BAKING BASICS

Batter is a curious word. It refers to an almost liquid mixture of flour with other ingredients, and we usually think of pancakes, waffles, or Yorkshire puddings when talking about recipes made with batter. However, there are so many more kinds of bread you can make with batter, and they are really easy to prepare, as they don't require kneading.

PANCAKES AND WAFFLES

Of course pancakes and waffles do not require yeast—natural or otherwise. Typically, they are made with bicarbonate of soda or baking powder, both of which act as the rising agent. However, pancakes and waffles made with sourdough are worth trying for a few reasons, and they don't require much more work than regular pancakes or waffles: they just take a bit of advanced planning. As the flour lies around doing its thing, it develops flavor, and the many hours it spends fermenting makes the resulting pancakes and waffles really easy to digest.

BATTER BREAD

To make batter bread, you simply spoon the batter into a pan and bake it. The resulting bread is similar to a "quick bread" or a "tea loaf." The loaves are moist and flavorful with a dense crumb that is more like a muffin than a loaf of bread. Batter breads make a wonderful alternative to "regular" bread and, as with the waffles and pancakes, the flavor is deliciously strong, and the bread is easy to digest.

The basic recipe that follows is for a totally plain batter bread. Alternatively, you can add anything you like to vary the flavor. This chapter includes a variation with cranberries and blueberries but you can add anything! Our favorites include walnuts and raisins; pumpkin seeds and sunflower seeds; grated Cheddar cheese and dry chili flakes; and sautéed onion and bacon. Simply make the bread and stir in a handful of any extra ingredients you like, and you will have delicious bread that is simple to make.

BASIC SOURDOUGH
BATTER BREAD

Makes about 2½ cups batter

1 cup (260 g) wheat sourdough starter
1½ cups (210 g) white wheat bread flour,
plus extra as needed
¼ cup (60 ml) cold water

½ tsp salt
1 tbsp sugar
1 tbsp melted butter
¼ cup (60 ml) milk

METHOD

Day one

1. Measure the sourdough starter into a large bowl and return any remaining starter to the refrigerator.
2. Add 1 cup (140 g) flour and the water, cover with plastic wrap and leave on the counter for 12 hours.

Day two

3. Add the salt, sugar, and butter to the milk and mix. Add to the refreshed starter and mix well. Add the remaining ½ cup (70 g) flour and mix well to make a batter.
4. Spoon the batter into a greased 4 x 8-inch (10 x 20 cm) loaf tin and cover with oiled plastic wrap. Proof at room temperature for 3 to 4 hours, until the dough has risen approximately ½ inch (13 mm) above the top of the loaf tin. Preheat the oven to 400°F (200°C).
5. Bake for 40 minutes.

STORING AND USING A SOURDOUGH STARTER

Once you have made your starter, you can use some immediately but don't use it all or you will need to make another batch before you bake again. It's important to hold some back for the next time you want to bake. In order to keep your starter and pass it down to your grandchildren, you need to care for it properly, and to do this you have two options.

OPTION 1: Keep your starter in a permanent state of refreshment

Realistically, if you are not baking in volume, this option is not really viable. You probably won't use enough starter to keep a manageable vat that stays lively. However, if you really want to feed the starter every day, give it a try. Just add enough flour and water to your starter to maintain its consistency. You may find that one of these things happens:

- The volume of starter gets increasingly bigger because you're not using it.
- The starter gets weaker as it gets older. This is because you have an increasingly large amount of starter to which you are adding a relatively small amount of new food. The yeast eats the new food in record time (you will see it froth almost instantly then an hour later it's calm again) and goes to sleep. Sleepy yeast does not make great bread, which is why some methods tell you to throw half your starter away on a regular basis. I'm against this method because I don't believe in wasting food.
- You forget about your starter and it dies.

Professional bakers use lots of starter and they put lots of flour and water back every day. Nevertheless, many of them put their starters in the refrigerator every night just in case.

OPTION 2: Refresh your starter when you need it

You can freeze your starter, you can dry your starter, you can refrigerate it in an airtight container, and it will just go to sleep. That way, you can ignore it until the next time you want to bake. What you can't do is leave it in a liquid state at room temperature much longer than a couple of days without feeding it. At room temperature the yeast will eventually eat everything in sight and then starve to death. At that point, the starter will go moldy and die. If your starter has mold on it, it is best to throw it away. I once found some starter in the back of the refrigerator that had been there for about five years. I refreshed it (which took two days), and it was as good as new.

To refresh the starter when you need it, simply follow the instructions in the recipe. The recipes in this book assume you will store your starter in the refrigerator and that it will need refreshing. To that end, they build in refreshment time, and you get used to planning this in advance. In five minutes you have taken out your starter and fed it, and then you can go to bed or go to work and pick up the process later.

If you kill your starter, it's not the end of the world, as you can make more in four days. It is not the same as running out of yeast—when that happens you have to find a shop and buy more. That obviously isn't an issue in the modern age, but it would have been if you were crossing Canada in a covered wagon a few hundred years ago. However, even if you had no starter and you happened to be transported back in time, the only implication of your foolishness is that you and your family would be forced to eat pancakes for four days until you made more starter. And that wouldn't exactly be a hardship.

STORING BREAD

Many kinds of sourdough bread (especially those with a high rye content) are very "damp" when they come out of the oven. You should wait until your bread is completely cool before cutting into it because the final structure of the crumb is still forming as the bread cools. You can certainly wait 24 to 48 hours before cutting into the bread and it will still be fantastic. After the bread is cool, and while you wait, simply wrap the loaf in a tea towel and leave it on the counter.

YUKON FLAPJACKS

- -

Make sure the pan is very hot before pouring on the batter. When bubbles start to appear and the edges go brown, it is time to turn the flapjacks over.

INGREDIENTS

1 cup (260 g) wheat sourdough starter
½ cup (70 g) white wheat bread flour
¼ cup (60 ml) water
¼ tsp salt
1 tbsp sugar
1 tbsp vegetable oil
1 egg, beaten

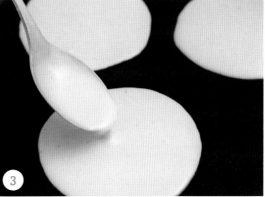

METHOD

Day one

1. Measure the sourdough starter into a large bowl and return any remaining starter to the refrigerator.
2. Mix in the flour and water, cover with plastic wrap, and leave on the counter for 12 hours.

Day two

3. Mix the remaining ingredients into the refreshed starter and mix well. Heat a large pan, and use a pitcher or ladle to pour the batter into the pan, forming 3-inch (7.5 cm) rounds.
4. Cook for 2 to 4 minutes, or until bubbles form on the surface and the edges go brown.
5. Turn over and cook for a further 2 minutes. Serve hot.

✿ TIPS

If the first flapjacks don't rise as much as desired, sieve ½ tsp baking soda into the remaining batter and whisk it in well just before cooking.

Batter Bread

29

CRANBERRY AND BLUEBERRY BATTER BREAD

Cranberries have become an increasingly popular ingredient in baking, and when partnered with fresh blueberries, the combination is hard to beat.

INGREDIENTS

1 cup (260 g) wheat sourdough starter
1½ cups (210 g) white wheat bread flour
1 cup (240 ml) water
½ tsp salt
1 tbsp sugar
1 tbsp butter, melted
¼ cup (60 ml) milk
½ cup (75 g) blueberries
½ cup (90 g) dried cranberries
¼ cup (30 g) flaked almonds, to sprinkle

METHOD

Day one

1. Measure the sourdough starter into a large bowl and return any remaining starter to the refrigerator.
2. Mix in 1 cup (140 g) flour and the water, cover with plastic wrap, and leave on the counter for 12 hours.

Day two

3. Combine the milk with the salt, sugar, and butter in a bowl. Add to the refreshed starter and mix well.
4. Sprinkle the remaining ½ cup (70 g) flour over the batter mix, scatter over the fruit and stir gently to mix. Spoon the batter into a greased 8 x 8-inch (20 x 20 cm) square loaf tin, cover with oiled plastic wrap, and proof at room temperature for 1½ to 2 hours. Preheat the oven to 400°F (200°C).
5. Sprinkle over the flaked almonds and bake for 40 minutes until risen and golden brown. If the loaf is becoming dark, cover with foil for the last 10 minutes of baking time.
6. Remove from the loaf tin and cool on a wire rack.

FLUFFY WAFFLES

As the name suggests, this recipe results in light, fluffy waffles that are perfect for breakfast.
Serve with maple syrup and fresh fruit.

 ## INGREDIENTS

1 cup (260 g) wheat sourdough starter
½ cup (60 g) spelt flour
¼ cup (35 g) white wheat bread flour
¼ cup (60 ml) water
1 cup (240 ml) cream
½ tsp baking powder
1 tbsp sugar
4 eggs, separated
½ cup (30 g) wheatgerm
¼ tsp salt
Huckleberries and maple syrup, to serve

METHOD

Day one

1. Measure the sourdough starter into a large bowl and return any remaining starter to the refrigerator.
2. Mix in the flour and water, cover with plastic wrap, and leave on the counter for 12 hours.

Day two

3. Mix the cream, baking powder, sugar, egg yolks, wheatgerm and salt into the refreshed starter and whisk well to remove any lumps. Preheat a waffle iron.
4. Beat the egg whites until they form soft peaks and gently fold into the batter.
5. Pour the batter onto the hot waffle iron and cook for 7 to 8 minutes, or according to the manufacturer's instructions. Repeat with the remaining batter. Serve hot.

SOUR CREAM WAFFLES

The addition of sour cream gives these waffles a rich flavor and fluffy texture. Serve with extra sour cream and sweet fruit compote.

INGREDIENTS

2 cups (520 g) wheat sourdough starter
1 cup (140 g) white wheat bread flour
½ cup (120 ml) water
1 cup (240 ml) sour cream
2 tbsp (30 g) butter, melted
1 tbsp (15 g) sugar
1 tsp (5 g) salt
2 eggs, separated
Maple syrup, cream, and fruit, to serve

METHOD

Day one

1. Measure the sourdough starter into a large bowl and return any remaining starter to the refrigerator.
2. Mix in the flour and water, cover with plastic wrap, and leave on the counter for 12 hours.

Day two

3. Mix the remaining ingredients, except the egg whites, into the refreshed starter. Preheat a waffle iron.
4. Beat the egg whites until they forms soft peaks and gently fold into the batter.
5. Pour the batter onto the waffle iron and cook for 7 to 8 minutes, or according to the manufacturer's instructions. Repeat with the remaining batter. Serve hot with maple syrup, cream and fresh fruit.

Batter Bread

EVERYDAY RYE

To successfully bake sourdough rye bread, begin by making a rye starter (see page 40). The Pure Rye recipe (see pages 44–45) is a good place to start, before moving onto the more challenging Peasant Bread (see pages 52–54) or Raisin Rye (see pages 62–65).

RYE BAKING BASICS

Rye is the staple bread in most of north and north eastern Europe, and Russia, for the simple reason that rye is the grain that traditionally grew in these regions. Wheat is a relatively recent crop, and while it is popular for bread baking, rye remains the dominant grain.

Rye bread has a wonderful flavor, is easy to work with and is delicious when paired with traditional, northern European foods (strong cheese, smoked, pickled and fermented fish, meat, and vegetables). Rye contains gluten but it is a different type of gluten than that found in wheat and the wheat family. The gluten in rye isn't stretchy, which means a couple of things:

1. You can't shape it the way you shape bread made with wheat flour: it just breaks if you pull on it.
2. It will never rise as high as dough made with wheat flour because the carbon dioxide bubbles that develop when the yeast gets to work eventually burst through the surface of the dough, as the fragile gluten breaks.
3. Your loaf will never have the high dome of bread made with wheat flour. Rye loaves are normally flatter than wheat loaves.
4. Your loaf will always be denser, with smaller bubbles, in a more closed crumb structure. However, the dense structure doesn't result in heavy, brick-like bread—if it is, your dough was probably too dry. Rye absorbs a lot of water and the dough should be soft and feel smooth. If the dough is dry and/or gritty, gradually add more water until it is soft and smooth.

KNEADING RYE DOUGH

Kneading dough with rye flour can be a challenge if you're not used to it. It has a texture that is both sticky and slimy. If you are making 100% rye bread you don't actually need to knead it at all. If you are mixing rye and wheat, however, the results will be better if you knead the dough in order to activate the stretchy gluten in the wheat flour.

Be prepared to get messy—you will find it easier if you use a scraper. Push the dough away from you with the heel of your hand and gather it back into a pile with the scraper. Repeat, repeat, repeat, adding more water, as necessary, if the dough becomes too hard and dry.

SHAPING RYE DOUGH

Shaping rye dough requires wet hands. Dough sticks to dough so, when you are ready to shape your dough, have a bowl of water beside you.

Gather the dough together in a ball in the bowl or on the counter with a scraper. Then, with very wet hands, scoop it up and pass it from hand to hand. Hold it in the right hand and smooth the surface with the left hand, then transfer it to the left hand and smooth the surface with the right hand. Try to keep the shape to the same size as the container and continue to smooth it until it is like a small brick or ball, depending on the recipe. When it is the right shape, gently place it in the container. Don't squash it to fit—the dough will rise and fill the corners.

BAKING RYE BREAD

Rye does not necessarily sound hollow when it is baked—sometimes it's just a bit too dense for that. However, the bottom crust will feel thin when you tap it, a bit like tapping an empty Tupperware. If you're concerned you won't get it right, buy a probe thermometer. The inside temperature of bread when it is baked is 208°F (98°C).

Finally, because dough made with rye flour is highly hydrated in order for the bread to be light, the bread is often damp. This is a double-edged sword: on the one hand, you really don't want to cut into rye bread until it is at least 24 hours old, which means you have to wait. On the other hand, it will be delicious, moist, and edible for 5 to 6 days—it really does stay fresh for ages. To store it, simply wrap it in a tea towel and put it in a bread crock made of tin, ceramic, or glass. That way it won't go moldy quickly either.

❧ FAST FACT: SLOWLY DOES IT

Many people believe sourdough bread to be healthier than other types of bread. However, it is not that sourdough bread is necessarily better for you—any long fermentation bread is better than bread that is fermented over a short time.

Bread rises because the yeast is eating the flour and breaking it down in a particular chemical process called fermentation. This process creates the gas that makes the dough rise. When bread dough goes through a long fermentation process, the flour is broken down more than during a short fermentation. So, the longer the bread takes to ferment, the easier it is to digest.

MAKING A RYE
SOURDOUGH STARTER

Day 1

Mix just under ½ cup (50 g) whole rye flour and ¾ cup (180 ml) water together in a large bowl. Cover with plastic wrap or place a dinner plate over the bowl, and put it on the counter for 24 hours.

Day 2

Add just under ½ cup (50 g) whole rye flour and ¾ cup (180 ml) water to the mix in the bowl. Stir, cover it and put it on the counter for 24 hours.

Day 3

Add just under ½ cup (50 g) whole rye flour and ¾ cup (180 ml) water to the mix in the bowl. Stir, cover it and put it on the counter for 24 hours.

Day 4

Add just under ½ cup (50 g) whole rye flour and ¾ cup (180 ml) water to the mix in the bowl. Stir, cover it and put it on the counter for 24 hours.

Day 5

Your starter should be bubbly—if it is, you have a viable starter. If not, don't add any more flour or water, just cover it and let it sit for another 24 hours. However, if nothing has happened by day six, it could be that your house is just too clean, or the air where you live is polluted and sadly lacking in natural yeast (very unusual but it happens). You could stop using bleach or antiseptic sprays on your kitchen surfaces, and revert to hot, soapy water for cleaning, and try again. Sourdough needs germs!

Your starter should be bubbly and lively: if it is, you're ready to start making sourdough bread; if not, put it down to experience and try again.

READY TO BAKE

You now have plenty of starter to use straight away in any recipe that calls for a rye starter. You also have plenty to put back into a container in the refrigerator to take out when you need it. When you put it back in the refrigerator use a large container, as your starter will continue to froth up before it calms down. If your container is too small, you might find starter all over the refrigerator the following morning. After a day or two it will calm down, go quiet, and separate into the liquid that floats on top and the sediment on the bottom.

THE GOLDEN RULE: DON'T RUN OUT OF STARTER

If you run out, will have to make another, or find a friend who has one. So, you can do one of two things:

1. When you are following a recipe you can refresh twice as much sourdough starter as the recipe calls for, and put what you don't need back in the container in the refrigerator.

2. When you get down to 1 cup (260 g) or so of starter in the refrigerator, simply top up the container. For every ½ cup (130 g) of rye starter in your container, add 1¼ cups (125 g) of rye flour and 2¼ cups (540 ml) of water. Mix, cover and leave on the counter overnight. You how now have a new container of bubbly rye starter.

TROUBLESHOOTING RYE BREAD

PROBLEM

Your bread is cracked along the side of the loaf where the dough meets the pan.

SOLUTION

You didn't leave it long enough before baking it. Carefully read the recipe instructions and follow them with regard to how rye should look before you bake it. Photograph your loaf before you put it in the oven: if your bread does crack, chalk it up to experience and leave it to rise longer (you'll see it's larger when you compare your next attempt to your photo).

PROBLEM

Your bread collapses in the middle and/or droops down the side of the pan.

SOLUTION

You left your bread for too long before you baked it. Rye dough should stand up straight coming out of the pan before you bake it. If it begins to droop over the side of the pan in folds, it has over-risen. If this happens, don't bake it—pull it out and wash and re-grease the pan, then re-shape your dough and put it back. It will bounce back pretty quickly so watch it and put it in the oven before it droops.

PROBLEM

The crust comes away from the crumb—you can see this when you cut into the bread.

SOLUTION

You left your bread for too long before you baked it. Underneath the crust, the crumb collapsed. This can be hard to spot so look for any signs of a somewhat collapsed or "wavy" surface on the dough before you bake it.

PROBLEM

Your bread is dense, brick-like, hard, and dry—you could use it as a doorstop.

SOLUTION

Your dough is too dry—it's that simple. I can't emphasize enough how wet your rye dough has to be, for it to bake into lovely bread. To test your dough, wet a finger and push it right through the dough with some force. Don't just prod or poke it, really push it right to the bottom so your finger makes contact with the bowl. Your finger should push through very easily and the dough should feel smooth, not gritty. Go beyond your comfort zone and you will soon develop the confidence to have really wet dough.

PROBLEM

Your bread is sticky and under-baked when you cut into it, even one or two days later.

SOLUTION

You have not baked the bread for long enough, your oven temperature is too low, you have used too much sourdough starter to fresh flour, or you have developed the dough over too long a timeframe. A probe thermometer is the answer to the first problem. The internal temperature of baked bread is 208°F (98°C). An oven thermometer is the answer to the second problem—even a few degrees can make a huge difference. If you are experimenting, adjust the ratios and shorten the "build" time.

PROBLEM

Your rye dough isn't rising.

SOLUTION

Rye can take ages to rise, especially on a cold, dark morning (6 to 8 hours if your kitchen is very cold). Be patient—as long as your sourdough starter was lively and bubbly when you put your dough together, the dough will rise. Make sure it is well covered (use a plastic shower cap) so it doesn't dry out. If you run out of time and your rye is not as risen as you would like, pop it in the refrigerator where it will continue to rise, albeit slowly. At 41°F (5°C)—the temperature of most refrigerators—rye takes 8 hours to rise, so you can sleep, go to work or go out for the day. Then simply take it out of the regrigerator, preheat the oven, and pop it in from cold: it works every time.

PROBLEM

Should you use dark or light rye?

SOLUTION

By convention, rye is labeled either "dark" or "light" rye, rather than "whole" or "white" rye: dark rye is like whole wheat, and light rye is like white wheat. That is to say, dark rye contains the bran and germ of the whole rye grain, whereas light rye has the bran and germ sieved out. This means that dark rye is heavier and has a strong, nutty flavor. Sometimes it takes longer to rise and it's denser than rye bread made with light rye. If you find your bread is too heavy for your tastes, try using light rye instead of dark, or just sieve the dark rye to remove the bran and germ (you can put this in your granola or sprinkle it on cereal or salad instead).

PROBLEM

Your bread is burning on the top before it is done.

SOLUTION

The problem may be the oven temperature—if your oven is running too high your bread may well burn on top. Check the temperature of your oven with a good-quality oven thermometer.

If your oven temperature is accurate, remember that extra ingredients such as nuts, and dried fruit will burn in the oven before your bread turns brown. Sugar will have an impact too: it caramelizes quickly, turning the crust of sweetened bread brown very quickly. When baking with extra ingredients and/or with sweetened dough, you may want to check your bread halfway through the baking time. If it is getting really brown, cover the top of the loaf with wax paper and continue baking. All will be well.

Makes a 1½ lb (675 g) loaf

PURE RYE

- -

This recipe produces a rich, dark loaf that is packed with flavor. As it contains only rye flour, it won't rise like a wheat loaf, and its dense structure means it's best served in thin slices.

INGREDIENTS

½ cup (130 g) rye sourdough starter
3¼ cups (325 g) rye flour
1½ cups (360 ml) water
1 tsp salt
¼ cup (25 g) rolled rye (or oats), for coating

 NOTE:

Once the loaf is in the proofing basket, it can be kept in the refrigerator up to 8 hours before baking.

METHOD

Day one

1. Put the sourdough starter in a large bowl and return any remaining starter to the refrigerator.
2. Add ¾ cup (75 g) rye flour, and ½ cup (120 ml) water, and stir gently to mix. Cover with plastic wrap, and leave on the counter for 8 hours or overnight.

Day two

3. Add the remaining ingredients, except the rolled rye, to the refreshed starter and mix well.
4. Pick up the dough with wet hands and shape into an oblong loaf. Pour the rolled rye or oats onto a plate and gently roll the loaf in them to coat it completely (use your fingers to coat the ends of the loaf).
5. Place in a very well-floured proofing basket, and cover with oiled plastic wrap. Proof at room temperature for 3 to 4 hours. Preheat the oven to 425°F (220°C).
6. Carefully invert the proofing basket to gently roll the loaf onto a floured baking sheet. Bake for 10 minutes, then reduce the temperature to 400°F (200°C), and bake for a further 20 to 25 minutes.

FINNISH RYE

- -

The addition of brown sugar gives this dense rye loaf a rich, golden color, but the white flour means it still has a fluffy texture. This is a popular bread in Scandinavian countries.

INGREDIENTS

¼ cup (65 g) rye sourdough starter
1½ cups (150 g) rye flour
1½ cups (210 g) white wheat bread flour
¾ cup (180 ml) water
½ cup (120 ml) milk
¾ tsp salt
⅓ cup (60 g) firmly packed brown sugar
1 tbsp butter, melted

TIP

It is important to shape the dough with wet hands, as this stops the dough from sticking to your hands. If your work surface isn't within easy reach of your sink, keep a bowl of water close by so you can keep your hands wet while you work with the dough.

METHOD

Day one

1. Put the sourdough starter in a large bowl and return any remaining starter to the refrigerator.
2. Add ½ cup (50 g) rye flour, ½ cup (70 g) white flour and ¼ cup (60 ml) water, and stir gently to mix. Cover with plastic wrap, and leave on the counter for 8 hours or overnight.

Day two

3. Add the remaining ingredients to the refreshed starter and mix well. Turn out onto a lightly floured surface and knead until smooth (about 10 minutes).
4. Shape the dough with wet hands, gently place into a greased loaf pan and cover with oiled plastic wrap. Proof at room temperature for 3 to 4 hours, until the dough has risen about 1 inch (2.5 cm) above the top of the loaf pan and has little holes in it. Preheat the oven to 425°F (220°C).
5. Bake for 10 minutes then reduce the temperature to 400°F (200°C), and bake for a further 30 to 35 minutes.
6. Remove from the loaf pan and cool on a wire rack. This bread is best eaten 1 to 2 days after it has been baked.

>> *See steps on page 48*

FINNISH RYE

4a

Shape the dough with wet hands and gently place in a greased loaf pan.

4b

Proof at room temperature, until the dough has risen about 1 inch (2.5 cm) above the rim of the loaf pan.

6

Remove from the loaf pan and cool on a wire rack.

LIGHT SWEDISH LIMPA

Limpa is a rye bread flavored with brown sugar or molasses, and the orange zest complements the light rye flavor. Use a coarse grater to produce large strips and chunks of the zest.

INGREDIENTS

1 cup (260 g) rye sourdough starter
1½ cups (210 g) white wheat bread flour
½ cup (50 g) rye flour
½ cup (120 ml) water
½ tsp salt
¼ cup (45 g) firmly packed brown sugar
1 tbsp butter
Grated zest of ½ orange
½ tbsp caraway seeds
1 tbsp fennel seeds

METHOD

Day one

1. Put the sourdough starter in a large bowl and return any remaining starter to the refrigerator.
2. Add ½ cup (70 g) white flour, all of the rye flour and ¼ cup (60 ml) water, and stir gently to mix. Cover with plastic wrap, and leave on the counter for 8 hours or overnight.

Day two

3. Add the remaining ingredients to the refreshed starter and mix well. Turn out onto a lightly floured surface and knead for about 10 minutes or until smooth.
4. Shape the dough with wet hands into a sausage shape, gently place into a greased loaf pan and cover with oiled plastic wrap. Proof at room temperature for 3 to 4 hours, until the dough has risen about 1 inch (2.5 cm) above the top of the loaf pan. Preheat the oven to 425°F (220°C).
5. Bake for 10 minutes then reduce the temperature to 400°F (200°C), and bake for a further 30 minutes.
6. Remove from the loaf pan and cool on a wire rack.

>> *See steps on page 50*

Everyday Rye

LIGHT SWEDISH LIMPA

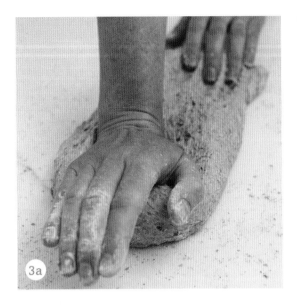

Turn out onto a lightly floured surface and knead until smooth.

This will take about 10 minutes.

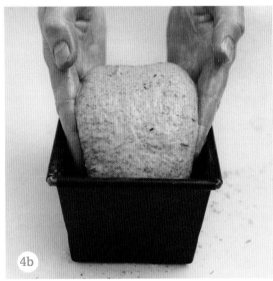

Shape the dough with wet hands into a sausage shape.

Gently place into a greased loaf pan.

Makes a 1½ lb (675 g) loaf

PEASANT BREAD

- -

The combination of coriander and molasses in this Russian recipe complements the sourdough flavor.

INGREDIENTS

1 cup (260 g) rye sourdough starter

½ cup (50 g) rye flour

½ cup (65 g) whole wheat bread flour, plus extra for dusting

½ cup (70 g) white wheat bread flour

½ cup (120 ml) water

½ tsp salt

¼ cup (60 ml) milk

1 tbsp dark molasses

1 tbsp vegetable oil

½ tsp ground coriander

TIP:

Before adding the milk to the ingredients, heat it to just below boiling point, then cool it to room temperature.

METHOD

Day one

1. Put the sourdough starter in a large bowl and return any remaining starter to the refrigerator.
2. Add the rye flour, the whole wheat flour, and the water, and stir gently to mix. Cover with plastic wrap, and leave on the counter for 8 hours or overnight.

Day two

3. Add the remaining ingredients to the refreshed starter and mix well. Turn out onto a lightly floured surface and knead until smooth (about 10 minutes).
4. Shape the dough into a ball. Gently place in a greased and floured round 9-inch (23 cm) baking pan (or round springform pan), and cover with oiled plastic wrap. Proof at room temperature for 3 to 4 hours, until the dough has risen about 1 inch (2.5 cm) above the top of the baking pan. Preheat the oven to 425°F (220°C).
5. Dust the loaf with flour. Bake for 10 minutes, then reduce the temperature to 400°F (200°C), and bake for a further 30 to 35 minutes.
6. Remove from the baking pan and cool on a wire rack.

>> *See steps on page 54*

PEASANT BREAD

Shape the dough into a ball.

Gently place it in a greased and floured baking pan.

Dust the loaf with flour.

Makes a 1½ lb (675 g) loaf

PUMPERNICKEL RYE

- -

Pumpernickel is a dark bread traditionally made with coarsely ground rye flour. If you cannot find pumpernickel flour, just use regular dark rye flour.

INGREDIENTS

1 cup (260 g) rye sourdough starter

1 cup (100 g) coarse pumpernickel flour
    or dark rye flour

1½ cups (210 g) white wheat bread flour

½ cup (120 ml) water

¾ tsp salt

1 tbsp sugar

½ cup (120 ml) milk

½ tbsp caraway seeds

1 tbsp vegetable oil

METHOD

Day one

1. Put the sourdough starter in a large bowl and return any remaining starter to the refrigerator.
2. Add ½ cup (50 g) pumpernickel flour, ½ cup (70 g) white flour and the water, and stir gently to mix. Cover with plastic wrap, and leave on the counter for 8 hours or overnight.

Day two

3. Add the remaining ingredients to the refreshed starter and mix well. Turn out onto a lightly floured surface and knead for about 10 minutes or until smooth.
4. Shape the dough with wet hands, gently place in a greased loaf pan and cover with oiled plastic wrap. Proof at room temperature for 3 to 4 hours, until the dough has risen about 1 inch (2.5 cm) above the top of the loaf pan. Preheat the oven to 425°F (220°C).
5. Bake for 10 minutes at 425°F (220°C), then reduce the temperature to 400°F (200°C), and bake for a further 30 to 35 minutes.
6. Remove from the loaf pan and cool on a wire rack.

>> *See steps on page 56*

PUMPERNICKEL RYE

Prepare the starter and leave overnight to refresh.

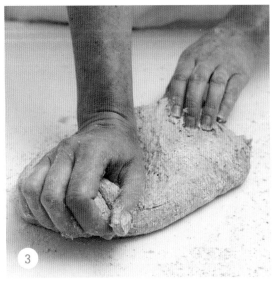

Turn out onto a lightly floured surface and knead.

Shape the dough with wet hands.

AUSTRIAN RYE AND WHEAT

The combination of white wheat and rye flours produces a moderate rye flavor. The bread rises well but results in a somewhat heavier loaf than all-wheat bread. The addition of anise and caraway impart flavors that are characteristic of a European rye loaf.

INGREDIENTS

1 cup (260 g) wheat sourdough starter

1 cup (100 g) rye flour

1 cup (140 g) white wheat bread flour

¼ cup (60 ml) water

½ cup (120 ml) milk

¾ tsp salt

1 tbsp sugar

½ tsp ground cumin

1 tsp caraway seeds, plus extra to decorate

½ tsp anise seeds, plus extra to decorate

METHOD

Day one

1. Put the sourdough starter in a large bowl and return any remaining starter to the refrigerator.
2. Add ½ cup (50 g) rye flour, ½ cup (70 g) white flour, and the water, and stir gently to mix. Cover with plastic wrap, and leave on the counter for 8 hours or overnight.

Day two

3. Add the remaining ingredients, except the seeds, to the refreshed starter and mix well. Turn out onto a lightly floured surface and knead until smooth (about 10 minutes).
4. Shape the dough into a tight sausage, gently place in a greased loaf pan, and cover with oiled plastic wrap. Proof at room temperature for 3 to 4 hours. Preheat the oven to 425°F (220°C).
5. Brush the loaf with water, scatter over the caraway and anise seeds, and slash the top in a criss-cross pattern. Bake for 10 minutes then reduce the temperature to 400°F (200°C), and bake for a further 30 to 35 minutes.
6. Remove from the loaf pan and cool on a wire rack.

DURUM RYE

The combination of different flours results in a rich-tasting bread, while the milk and brown sugar add a hint of sweetness.

INGREDIENTS

¼ cup (65 g) rye sourdough starter
1 cup (140 g) durum flour
1 cup (140 g) white wheat bread flour
½ cup (50 g) rye flour
¾ cup (180 ml) water
½ cup (120 ml) milk
1 tsp salt
2 tbsp firmly packed brown sugar
1 tbsp melted butter or vegetable oil

METHOD

Day one

1. Put the sourdough starter in a large bowl and return any remaining starter to the refrigerator.
2. Add the durum flour and the water, and stir gently to mix. Cover with plastic wrap, and leave on the counter for 8 hours or overnight.

Day two

3. Add the remaining ingredients to the refreshed starter and mix well. Turn out onto a lightly floured surface and knead until smooth (about 10 minutes).
4. Shape the dough into a tight ball, place on a heavily floured baking sheet, and cover with oiled plastic wrap. Proof at room temperature for 3 to 4 hours. Preheat the oven to 425°F (220°C).
5. Dust the loaf with flour and cut 3 slashes across the top. Bake for 10 minutes then reduce the temperature to 400°F (200°C), and bake for a further 20 to 25 minutes.
6. Remove from the baking sheet and cool on a wire rack.

RAISIN RYE

- -

This is excellent bread for breakfast toast. For variety, substitute 1½ cups (190 g) whole wheat flour for the cup of rye flour and use 2 tbsp brown sugar instead of granulated sugar.

INGREDIENTS

2 cups (460 g) rye sourdough starter
1 cup (100 g) rye flour
½ cup (120 ml) water
2 cups (280 g) white wheat bread flour
1 tsp salt
½ tbsp sugar
½ tbsp oil
1 cup (170 g) raisins, plumped
   (see page 104)

For the glaze:
½ beaten egg
½ tbsp milk

METHOD

Day one

1. Put the sourdough starter in a large bowl and return any remaining starter to the refrigerator.
2. Add the rye flour and the water, and stir gently to mix. Cover with plastic wrap, and leave on the counter for 8 hours or overnight.

Day two

3. Add the remaining ingredients (except the raisins) to the refreshed starter and mix well. Turn out onto a lightly floured surface and knead until smooth (about 10 minutes).
4. Cover the dough with oiled plastic wrap and let it rest for 1 hour.
5. Form the dough into a ball. Pat or roll it into a flat oval and carefully squeeze in the raisins. Fold the top edge all the way over to meet the bottom edge, then gently cup your hand over the dough, and seal the edges by firmly pressing down.
6. Place the loaf seam-side down on a floured baking sheet and cover with oiled plastic wrap. Proof at room temperature for 3 to 4 hours. Preheat the oven to 425°F (220°C).
7. Combine the ingredients for the glaze and brush onto the loaf. Bake for 10 minutes, then reduce the temperature to 400°F (200°C), and bake for a further 20 to 25 minutes.
8. Remove from the baking sheet and cool on a wire rack.

>> *See steps on pages 64–65*

RAISIN RYE

Pat or roll it into a flat oval and carefully squeeze in the raisins.

Fold the top edge all the way over to meet the bottom edge.

Seal the edges by firmly pinching.

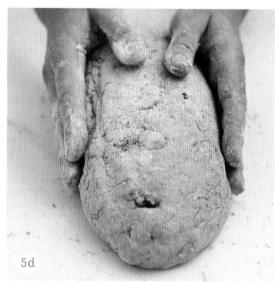

Shape the dough with wet hands into a rectangular loaf.

Place the loaf seam-side down on a floured baking sheet.

Combine the ingredients for the glaze and brush onto the loaf.

❧ FAST FACT: READ THE LABEL

Not all bread that is sold as sourdough is "pure" sourdough bread, but is made in an industrial process with the addition of sourdough powders that mimic the flavor of sourdough bread. Always read the label, ask the bakery, and do your homework. A pure sourdough loaf will take most of a day to prepare and bake.

CARAWAY SPELT

Spelt produces a rich, creamy texture when added to a sourdough starter, and the difference between spelt flour and wheat flours is immediately obvious. The unique flavor of caraway is a perfect partnership with spelt.

INGREDIENTS

1 cup (260 g) rye sourdough starter
1 cup (100 g) rye flour
1¼ cups (125 g) white spelt flour
½ cup (120 ml) water
¾ tsp salt
1 tbsp butter, melted
1 tbsp dark molasses
1 tbsp caraway seeds

METHOD

Day one

1. Measure the sourdough starter into a large bowl and return any remaining starter to the refrigerator.
2. Add ½ cup (50 g) rye flour, ½ cup (50 g) spelt flour, and the water, and stir gently to mix. Cover with plastic wrap, and leave on the counter for 8 hours or overnight.

Day two

3. Add the remaining ingredients to the refreshed starter and mix well. Turn out onto a lightly floured surface and knead until smooth (about 10 minutes).
4. Shape the dough into a tight oval, place in a well-floured proofing basket, and cover with oiled plastic wrap. Proof at room temperature for 3 to 4 hours. Preheat the oven to 425°F (220°C).
5. Turn the dough out onto a floured baking sheet and slash the top.
6. Bake for 10 minutes, then reduce the temperature to 400°F (200°C), and bake for a further 30 to 35 minutes.
7. Remove from the baking sheet and cool on a wire rack.

EVERYDAY WHEAT

Here you'll find a recipe for San Francisco Sourdough (see pages 74–75), the best-known of all sourdough breads. Prepare the wheat starter on page 71 then try your hand at making this iconic loaf.

WHEAT BAKING BASICS

A BRIEF HISTORY OF WHEAT

Wheat is consistently one of the top three crops grown in the world, and the story of wheat, and how it came to be grown so widely, and in such volume is fascinating. The grasses from which modern wheat has been derived originated somewhere between what are now eastern Armenia and western Turkey. These "goat grasses" were probably hybridised by early farmers as long ago as 10,000 years, improving their yields and their resistance to weather and insects. Over the millennia the grains they have produced include einkorn, emmer, spelt, and the various strains of wheat that are gown today.

The story of wheat is the story of exploration and exodus. As humans have travelled, crops have spread, and wheat has proven itself to be a very adaptable crop. It is nutritious, flexible, and contains a kind of stretchy protein called gluten that allows it—when incorporated into bread dough—to rise into a light, airy crumb and to be stretched so that the baker can manipulate the dough into beautiful shapes, exercising his or her creativity and delighting the eye.

GLUTEN

A great deal has been written in the past ten years about the rise of gluten intolerances and celiac disease. There is no doubt this is happening and that many people feel better when they stop eating wheat and other grains that contain gluten. What is not clear, however, is exactly why this is happening. What sourdough bakers know for sure is that people who suffer discomfort when they eat industrially produced bread, don't necessarily experience this when they eat long-fermented bread.

The gluten in wheat and its cousins (einkorn, emmer, spelt, and kamut) is stretchy. "Hard," "strong," or "high-protein" flour will make a dough that is very stretchy and strong, whereas "soft," "all-purpose," "cake and pastry," or "low-protein" flour will make a dough that is more fragile. Bread made with hard flour will rise higher because the gluten will stretch out more before it begins to collapse. It will also be chewier. Bread made with soft flour will not rise as much and will be softer in the mouth. In general, hard wheat flour is stronger than spelt, einkorn, emmer or kamut but that is not always the case. There are farmers who grow remarkable spelt that is easily stronger and more absorbent than most wheat flour.

SWITCHING FLOUR

You can substitute spelt, emmer, einkorn, or kamut for wheat flour in any recipe, but remember that the texture of the dough, and the look, feel, and taste of the final product will be different. I suggest you follow recipes to the letter at first and try to memorise what the dough feels like—how sticky, how stretchy, how damp etc. Then, by all means, swap in different kinds of flour. Remember, that different brands of flour, and different bags of the same brand will vary, and will require slightly different amounts of water to get the dough to the desired texture. Similarly, changing grains will mean you need to adjust the recipe slightly.

KNEADING WHEAT BREAD

As you knead dough with wheat (or wheat family) flour, the dough transforms from a ragged mass to a stretchy, soft, pillowy delight. However, this usually takes a good 10 minutes or more of hard work. Remember that kneading is just stretching—like you stretch a balloon before you blow it up—and you need to stretch out your dough so the carbon dioxide created by the yeast can expand the dough. A scraper can help gather dough back after stretching.

MAKING A WHEAT SOURDOUGH STARTER

Day 1

Mix 1 cup (140 g) white wheat bread flour and 1 cup (240 ml) water together in a large bowl. Cover with plastic wrap or place a dinner plate on top of the bowl, and put it on the counter for 24 hours.

Day 2

Add 1 cup (140 g) white wheat bread flour and 1 cup (240 ml) water to the mix in the bowl. Stir, cover it, and put it on the counter for 24 hours.

Day 3

Add 1 cup (140 g) white wheat bread flour and 1 cup (240 ml) water to the mix in the bowl. Stir, cover it, and put it on the counter for 24 hours.

Day 4

Add 1 cup (140 g) white wheat bread flour and 1 cup (240 ml) water to the mix in the bowl. Stir, cover it, and put it on the counter for 24 hours.

Day 5

Your starter should be bubbly—if it is, you have a viable starter. If not, don't add any more flour or water, just cover it, and let it sit for another 24 hours. However, if nothing has happened by day six, it is unlikely that your starter will be a success this time around. Chalk it up to experience, rinse out the bowl, and try again. Very occasionally, in some locations, the air is polluted and sadly lacking in natural yeast. Another uncommon (but entirely possible) reason is that your house is too clean. Sourdough needs germs!

READY TO BAKE

You now have plenty of starter to use straight away in any recipe that calls for a wheat starter. Or you can pick up the recipe with the quantity of "refreshed" starter that is called for. You also have plenty to put back into a container in the refrigerator to take out when you need it. When you put it back in the refrigerator use a large container, as your starter will continue to froth up before it calms down. If your container is too small, you will find starter all over the refrigerator. After a day or two it will stop frothing and separate into the liquid that floats on top and the sediment on the bottom.

Your starter should be bubbly and lively; you will notice that small bubbles start to appear after a couple of days.

TROUBLESHOOTING WHEAT BREAD

PROBLEM

Your bread is dense, brick-like, hard, and dry—you could use it as a doorstop.

SOLUTION

Your dough is too dry—it's that simple. Sourdough bread dough is a lot wetter and stickier than "regular" bread dough. To test your dough, pick up the dough and hold it by the edge. It should easily stretch a lot just through gravity. If it doesn't, add more liquid. You will soon develop the confidence and experience to have really wet dough.

PROBLEM

Your bread is cracked along the side of the loaf where the dough meets the pan.

SOLUTION

You didn't leave the dough for long enough before baking it. When proofing your dough, do the finger probe test before you bake it (see page 73). Proofing times vary with ingredients and weather conditions, and again, with experience you will be able to judge your dough better. It is important to recognise when dough is under-proofed, as a little extra proofing will save your finished loaf.

PROBLEM

Your bread collapses in the middle and/or droops down the side of the pan.

SOLUTION

You left your bread for too long before you baked it. Although dough can take different amounts of time to proof in different conditions, it's still perfectly possibly to overproof your dough. Again, you should do the finger probe test (see page 73) to check your dough is ready for baking.

PROBLEM
The crust comes away from the crumb—something you can see when you cut into it.
SOLUTION
You left your bread too long before you baked it—see solution on the previous page.

PROBLEM
Your bread is sticky and under-baked when you cut into it, even one or two days later.
SOLUTION
You have not baked the bread long enough, your oven temperature is too low, you have used too much sourdough starter to fresh flour, or you have developed the dough over too long a timeframe.

A probe thermometer is the simple answer to the first problem. The internal temperature of baked bread is 208°F (98°C). An oven thermometer will solve the second problem—even a few degrees can make a huge difference to how your bread turns out.

PROBLEM
Your wheat dough doesn't rise much in the time indicated by the recipe.
SOLUTION
Yeast is sensitive to hot and cold, and natural yeast is particularly sensitive: what could take 3 hours to rise at 75°F (24°C) could take 5 or 6 hours to rise at 70°F (21°C). To that end, the timings given in the recipes are a guide, and most of them reflect the temperature in a warm kitchen. You will know when your wheat sourdough bread is ready for the oven when it has grown by one-and-a-half times, and passed the finger probe test. Sourdough bread rarely grows more than that so don't expect it.

Use the finger probe test to check if your bread is ready for the oven. Poke the dough firmly with your finger to make an indentation: if your finger goes straight through, your bread is over-proofed (in which case, give it a little knead with more flour, reshape it and let it rise again). If the indentation remains for a minute or more, the bread should proof for a little longer. If the indentation springs back within a minute, the dough is ready for the oven.

The only temperature-controlled place in most homes is the refrigerator and this is a fail-safe way to proof your bread. Simply cover it and put it in the refrigerator for about 8 hours. Your refrigerator may be a little colder, and proofing will take longer, or a little less cold, and proofing will take less time. If, the first time you try this, your bread is over- or under-proofed, you know what to do the next time.

SAN FRANCISCO SOURDOUGH

- -

This is the best known of all sourdough breads and the one you're likely to see on display at farmers' markets and artisan bakers.

INGREDIENTS

⅓ cup (85 g) wheat sourdough starter
3⅔ cups (415 g) unbleached all-purpose flour
1⅓ cups (320 ml) water
1½ tsp salt

METHOD

Day one

1. Put the sourdough starter in a large bowl and return any remaining starter to the refrigerator.
2. Add ⅓ cup (40 g) flour and ⅓ cup (80 ml) water and mix. Cover with plastic wrap, and leave on the counter for 8 hours or overnight.

Day two

3. Add the remaining ingredients to the refreshed starter and mix well. Turn out onto a lightly floured surface and knead until smooth (about 10 minutes). Cover with plastic wrap and proof at room temperature overnight.

Day three

4. Shape the dough into a tight ball and gently place it in a large, round, well-floured proofing basket. Cover with oiled plastic wrap and proof at room temperature for 2½ to 4 hours. Preheat the oven to 425°F (220°C).
5. Invert the proofing basket to turn the dough out onto a floured baking sheet and slash the top of the loaf. Bake for 10 minutes then reduce the temperature to 400°F (200°C), and bake for a further 30 to 35 minutes.
6. Remove from the baking sheet and cool on a wire rack.

WHOLE WHEAT BREAD

A classic whole wheat loaf that includes milk for a richer flavor. Be sure to heat and cool your milk before using it in the recipe (see page 126).

INGREDIENTS

1 cup (260 g) wheat sourdough starter
1 cup (125 g) whole wheat bread flour
1½ cups (210 g) white wheat bread flour
⅓ cup (80 ml) water
1 tsp salt
½ cup (120 ml) warm milk
1 tbsp sugar
1 tbsp melted butter

METHOD

Day one

1. Measure the sourdough starter into a large bowl and return any remaining starter to the refrigerator.
2. Add ½ cup (65 g) whole wheat flour, ½ cup (70 g) white flour and the water, and stir gently to mix. Cover with plastic wrap and leave on the counter for 8 hours or overnight.

Day two

3. Add the remaining ingredients to the refreshed starter and mix well. Turn out onto a lightly floured surface and knead until smooth (about 10 minutes).
4. Shape the dough into a tight sausage, gently place in a well-floured oval proofing basket and cover with oiled plastic wrap. Proof at room temperature for 2½ to 4 hours. Preheat the oven to 425°F (220°C).
5. When ready to bake, invert the proofing basket to gently turn the dough out onto a floured baking sheet and slash, if liked. Bake for 10 minutes then reduce the temperature to 400°F (200°C), and bake for a further 30 to 35 minutes.
6. Remove from the baking sheet and cool on a wire rack.

MIXED GRAIN LOAF

Spelt is an ancient grain that makes an excellent addition to many sourdough breads. This recipe is made with white spelt and rye flours, but you could also use spelt in whole wheat breads, or as a substitute for rye in rye breads.

INGREDIENTS

1⅓ cups (350 g) sourdough starter
1⅓ cups (130 g) white spelt flour
1 cup (100 g) white wheat bread flour
¾ cup (180 ml) water
¾ tsp salt
1 tbsp sugar
2 tbsp vegetable oil
1 tbsp caraway seeds

METHOD

Day one

1. Put the sourdough starter in a large bowl and return any remaining starter to the refrigerator.
2. Add ½ cup (65 g) spelt flour, ½ cup (50 g) rye flour and the water, and stir gently to mix. Cover with plastic wrap and leave on the counter for 8 hours or overnight.

Day two

3. Add the remaining ingredients to the refreshed starter and mix well. Turn out onto a lightly floured surface and knead until smooth (about 10 minutes).
4. Shape the dough with wet hands into a tight sausage and gently place in a greased loaf pan. Proof at room temperature for 3 to 4 hours, until the dough has risen about 1 inch (2.5 cm) above the top of the loaf pan. Preheat the oven to 425°F (220°C).
5. Bake for 10 minutes then reduce the temperature to 400°F (200°C), and bake for a further 30 to 35 minutes.
6. Remove from the loaf pan and cool on a wire rack.

DO-GOOD LOAF

This is a variation of a recipe that was developed by Dr. Clive McCay at Cornell University in the 1940s. It was dubbed the Do-Good Loaf by Jean Hewitt in the New York Times Sunday Magazine.

INGREDIENTS

¼ cup (65 g) wheat sourdough starter
3½ cups (490 g) white wheat bread flour
1 cup (240 ml) water
¼ cup (30 g) non-fat dry milk
¾ tsp salt
1 tbsp brown sugar
1 tbsp vegetable oil
¾ tbsp wheatgerm

METHOD

Day one

1. Put the sourdough starter in a large bowl and return any remaining starter to the refrigerator.
2. Add 1 cup (140 g) white flour and ½ cup (120 ml) water, and stir gently to mix. Cover with plastic wrap and leave on the counter for 8 hours or overnight.

Day two

3. Add the remaining ingredients to the refreshed starter and mix well. Turn out onto a lightly floured surface and knead until smooth (about 10 minutes).
4. Shape into a tight sausage and gently place in a greased loaf pan, or shape into a free-form loaf on a floured baking sheet. Cover with oiled plastic wrap. Proof at room temperature for 2½ to 4 hours. Preheat the oven to 425°F (220°C).
5. Bake for 10 minutes, then reduce the temperature to 400°F (200°C), and bake for a further 30 to 35 minutes.
6. Remove from the baking sheet and cool on a wire rack.

PITA BREAD

- -

These soft, flat rounds with a pouch inside are produced throughout the Middle East, both commercially and in the home. It is a joy to watch the pita rounds start to puff up in the oven.

INGREDIENTS

1 cup (260 g) wheat sourdough starter
1 cup (140 g) white wheat bread flour
1 cup (125 g) whole wheat bread flour
½ cup (120 ml) water
¾ tsp salt
½ tbsp sugar
½ tbsp oil
Cornmeal or semolina, to sprinkle

METHOD

Day one

1. Put the sourdough starter in a large bowl and return any remaining starter to the refrigerator.
2. Add ½ cup (70 g) white flour, ½ cup (65 g) whole wheat bread flour, and the water, and stir gently to mix. Cover with plastic wrap and leave on the counter for 8 hours or overnight.

Day two

3. Add the remaining ingredients to the refreshed starter and mix well. Turn out onto a lightly floured surface and knead until smooth (about 10 minutes).
4. Divide the dough into 4 equal balls, and roll out to ¼-inch (5 mm) thick rounds on a well-floured surface. Place on a floured baking sheet, cover with oiled plastic wrap and proof at room temperature for 1½ hours.
5. Preheat the oven, and a baking stone or baking sheet, to 500°F (260°C). If using a baking stone, sprinkle the hot stone with cornmeal or semolina.

Use a large spatula to slide the rounds onto the stone, taking care not to damage the surface of the rounds. Cook in batches of 1 or 2 pitas. If using a baking sheet, remove the sheet from the oven, sprinkle on the cornmeal or semolina, and carefully place the rounds on the sheet before putting it back in the oven.

6. Bake for about 5 to 10 minutes, or until the rounds puff and start to brown. Remove from the oven with a spatula and cool on wire racks.

Makes 2 loaves

CIABATTA

- -

Ciabatta is made with a very soft, wet dough that can be tricky to handle. The shaping is almost like folding a slippery piece of cloth. Use plenty of flour at the shaping stages, and work quickly so the dough doesn't have time to stick to you, the counter, or your scraper. The wheat starter must be white for this recipe.

INGREDIENTS

¼ cup (65 g) wheat sourdough starter
4 cups (560 g) white wheat bread flour
4 cups (960 ml) water
1 tsp salt
Semolina or polenta, to sprinkle

METHOD

Day one

1. Measure the sourdough starter into a large bowl and return any remaining starter to the refrigerator.
2. Add 1 cup (140 g) flour and ¾ cup (180 ml) water and stir gently to mix. Cover with plastic wrap and leave on the counter for 8 hours or overnight.

Day two

3. Add the remaining ingredients to the refreshed starter and mix well. Turn out onto a lightly floured surface and knead until smooth, using a scraper (about 15 to 20 minutes). The dough will be very sticky and stringy.
4. Transfer the dough to a large bowl, cover with oiled plastic wrap, and proof at room temperature for 2½ to 3 hours.

5. Transfer the dough to a well-floured surface and flour the top. Using a dough scraper, divide into 2 pieces.
6. Take the first piece and gently stretch it out into a rectangle. Pick up the top edge (a scraper will help), and gently stretch it out and fold it two-thirds of the way over the rest of the rectangle. Gently place it down. Take the bottom edge, gently stretch it out and fold it almost over the top of the rest of the rectangle, then gently place it down. You should have what looks like a piece of paper folded for a business letter.
7. Using the scraper, carefully transfer the loaves to a heavily floured linen cloth (see page 19) and proof at room temperature for 1 hour. Preheat the oven to 500°F (250°C).
8. Heat a large baking sheet, and just before baking, remove it from the oven and sprinkle with semolina or polenta. Carefully transfer the loaves onto the sheet—they are more robust than they look but you need to work quickly.
9. Bake for 15 to 20 minutes. During the first 10 minutes of baking, spray a little water into the oven with a plant mister 2 or 3 times to increase the humidity.

>> *See steps on pages 84–85*

CIABATTA

Transfer the dough to a large bowl.

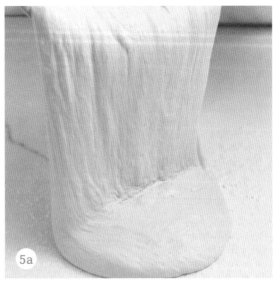

Transfer the dough to a well-floured surface and flour the top.

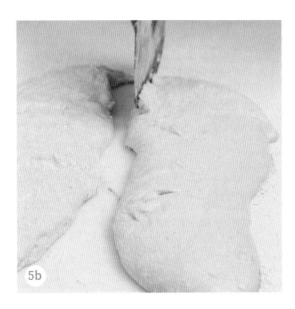

Using a dough scraper, divide into two pieces.

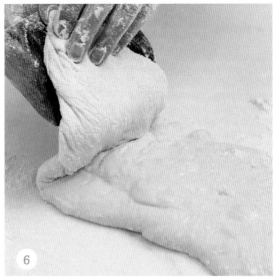

Pick up the top edge (a scraper will help), and gently stretch it out and fold it two-thirds of the way over the rest of the rectangle.

6a

Take the bottom edge, gently stretch it out and fold it almost over the top of the rest of the rectangle.

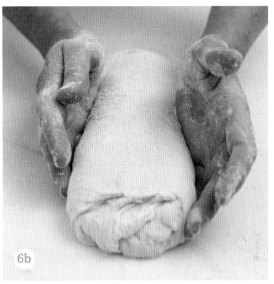

6b

You should have what looks like a piece of paper folded for a business letter.

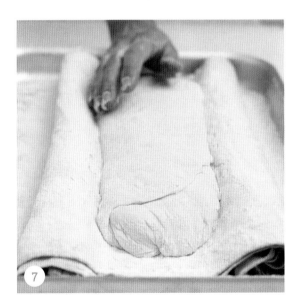

7

Carefully transfer the loaves to a heavily floured linen cloth.

❧ BAKING WHEAT BREAD

Wheat bread sounds "hollow" when it is baked. In addition, the bottom crust feels "thin" when you tap it. It will feel like you're tapping an empty plastic container; not one that is full of mashed potato. If you are concerned you won't get it right, buy a probe thermometer. The inside temperature of bread when it is baked is 208°F (98°C).

Finally, because sourdough bread dough is often more humid than "regular" bread dough (wet dough rises more quickly and easily than dry dough and the relatively weak yeast in sourdough needs all the help it can get) your bread may be damper than you are used to. If it is, and you don't like it, wrap it in a tea towel and let it dry out for a day before you use it.

KAMUT BREAD

Kamut is a cousin of wheat. It is considered an ancient grain and the gluten is weaker than strong wheat flour, so don't expect a big rise or lots of strong stretchiness.

INGREDIENTS

1 cup (260 g) wheat sourdough starter
1 cup (140 g) white wheat bread flour
¾ cup (180 ml) water
½ cup (50 g) rye flour
½ cup (60 g) kamut flour
¾ tsp salt
1 tbsp sugar
2 tbsp vegetable oil
1 tbsp caraway seeds
Milk, for brushing

METHOD

Day one

1. Measure the sourdough starter into a large bowl and return any remaining starter to the refrigerator.
2. Add the white flour and the water, and stir gently to mix. Cover with plastic wrap and leave on the counter for 8 hours or overnight.

Day two

3. Add the remaining ingredients to the refreshed starter and mix well. Turn out onto a lightly floured surface and knead until smooth (about 10 minutes).
4. Shape the dough into a tight sausage, gently place in a greased loaf pan and cover with oiled plastic wrap. Proof at room temperature for 2½ to 4 hours, until the dough rises about 1 inch (2.5 cm) above the top of the loaf pan. Preheat the oven to 425°F (220°C).
5. Brush the top of the loaf with milk. Bake for 10 minutes, then reduce the temperature to 400°F (200°C), and bake for a further 30 to 35 minutes.
6. Remove from the loaf tin and cool on a wire rack.

Makes a 1½ lb (675 g) loaf

WORLD BREAD

This simple loaf is a go-to for breakfast toast and lunchtime sandwiches. The milk helps to produce a light, fluffy texture.

INGREDIENTS

¼ cup (65 g) wheat sourdough starter
3 cups (420 g) white wheat bread flour
¾ cup (180 ml) water
½ cup (120 ml) milk
¾ tsp salt
1 tbsp sugar
½ tbsp melted butter

METHOD

Day one

1. Measure the sourdough starter into a large bowl and return any remaining starter to the refrigerator.
2. Add 1 cup (140 g) flour, and the water, and stir gently to mix. Cover with plastic wrap and leave on the counter for 8 hours or overnight.

Day two

3. Add the remaining ingredients to the refreshed starter and mix well. Turn out onto a lightly floured surface and knead until smooth (about 10 minutes).
4. Shape into a tight sausage and gently place in a greased loaf pan (or shape a tight ball or sausage to proof freely on a floured baking sheet), and cover with oiled plastic wrap. Proof at room temperature for 2½ to 4 hours. Preheat the oven to 425°F (220°C).
5. Bake for 10 minutes, then reduce the temperature to 400°F (200°C), and bake for a further 30 to 35 minutes.
6. Remove from the loaf pan and cool on a wire rack.

FRENCH BREAD

- -

Sourdough breads fell out of favor in French cities after the turn of the Twentieth Century when commercial yeast became available. However, they are now popular again and prevail in the country's smaller bakeries.

INGREDIENTS

2 cups (520 g) wheat sourdough starter
4¾ cups (665 g) white wheat bread flour
1¼ cups (300 ml) water
1 tsp salt

METHOD

Day one

1. Measure the sourdough starter into a large bowl and return any remaining starter to the refrigerator.
2. Add 2 cups (280 g) flour and the water, and stir gently to mix. Cover with plastic wrap and leave on the counter for 8 hours or overnight.

Day two

3. Add the remaining ingredients to the refreshed starter and mix well. Turn out onto a lightly floured surface and knead until smooth (about 10 minutes).
4. Divide the dough in half and form each piece into a long baguette shape. Place in a floured linen cloth (see page 19) to ensure even proofing. Proof at room temperature for 2½ to 4 hours. Preheat the oven to 425°F (220°C).
5. Just before baking, slash the dough several times diagonally along each loaf, and place on a floured baking sheet. Bake for 10 minutes then reduce the temperature to 400°F (200°C), and bake for a further 20 to 25 minutes.
6. Remove from the baking sheet and cool on a wire rack.

ENGLISH MUFFINS

- -

Sourdough English muffins are the perfect accompaniment to Eggs Benedict. The sourdough makes them tangy, and chewy, and they are delicious toasted.

INGREDIENTS

¼ cup (65 g) wheat sourdough starter
3¼ cups (455 g) white wheat bread flour
¾ cup (180 ml) water
½ cup (120 ml) milk
1 tsp salt
1½ tbsp melted butter
White cornmeal, for dusting

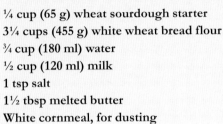

>> *See steps on page 92*

METHOD

Day one

1. Measure the sourdough starter into a large bowl and return any remaining starter to the refrigerator.
2. Add 2 cups (280 g) flour, and the water, and stir gently to mix. Cover with plastic wrap and leave on the counter for 8 hours or overnight.

Day two

3. Add the remaining ingredients to the refreshed starter and mix well. Turn out onto a lightly floured surface and knead until smooth (about 10 minutes).
4. Roll the dough on a floured surface into a flat oval that is approximately ½ inch (1 cm) thick. Using a 4-inch (10 cm) cookie cutter, cut out 10 muffins. Flour the cutter between cuts and avoid twisting the cutter as you pull it back out of the dough. (Alternatively, you can use the lid of an empty can or glass of the same diameter.)
5. Lightly grease a baking sheet and dust with white cornmeal. Place the muffins on the prepared sheet and dust with flour or cornmeal. Cover with a tea towel and proof at room temperature for 3 hours.
6. Preheat a large electric griddle to 400°F (200°C). Cook the muffins for 2 minutes, until browned underneath. Reduce the heat to 325°F (160°C), turn the muffins over, and cook on the other side for 8 minutes. Turn them again and cook for a further 6 minutes. Alternatively, you can bake the muffins in a preheated oven at 450°F (232°C) for 15 minutes.
7. Once cooked, transfer to wire racks to cool.

ENGLISH MUFFINS

4a

4b

Roll out the dough on a floured surface into a flat oval that is approximately ½ inch (1 cm) thick.

Using a 4-inch (10 cm) cookie cutter, cut out 10 muffins, and clear the cutter between cuts.

5

Lightly grease a baking sheet and dust with white cornmeal. Place the muffins on the prepared sheet and dust with flour or cornmeal.

BEIJING SESAME BUNS (SHAOBING)

Shaobing are traditional baked sesame buns that are crisp on the outside and tender on the inside. They are popular throughout northern and western China—you'll find them everywhere, from street vendors to high-end restaurants. You can buy sesame paste and Sichuan peppercorns at Chinese grocery stores. For a variation, replace the sesame paste with peanut butter.

INGREDIENTS

For the dough:
½ cup (130 g) wheat sourdough starter
3½ cups (490 g) white wheat bread flour
1 cup (240 ml) water
½ tsp salt

For the filling:
1 tsp Sichuan peppercorns
½ tsp fennel seeds
3 tbsp roasted sesame paste
1 tbsp toasted sesame oil
¼ tsp salt
4 tbsp sesame seeds, to sprinkle

METHOD

1. Combine the sourdough starter, flour, water, and salt in a large bowl, and knead for 10 minutes until the dough is smooth and pliable. Cover with plastic wrap and leave on the counter for 2 hours.

2. Toast the Sichuan peppercorns and fennel seeds in a pan and grind to a powder. Place in a mixing bowl and add the remaining filling ingredients. If it is too dry, add more sesame oil—the consistency should be like stiff syrup, not too runny.

3. Turn the dough out onto a lightly floured surface, pat into a rectangle, and roll out until it is about ⅛ inch (3 mm) thick, and twice as long as it is wide. You will have to pause for the dough to rest, stretching it again with your hands, if necessary, and re-flouring the surface to prevent sticking.

4. Spread the sesame filling over the dough, leaving a 1-inch (2.5 cm) margin along 1 long side. Starting with the opposite edge, roll up the dough. Finish by brushing a little water on the margin, and seal the roll.

5. Slice the dough into 3-inch (7.5 cm) long rounds. Taking 1 segment, pinch each end closed, then stand it upright and gently flatten it into a disc, patting it out so that it is about ¾ inch (2 cm) tall and 3½ inches (9 cm) wide.

6. Place the sesame seeds on a small plate. Brush each bun with a little water, and gently press the top and bottom into the seeds. Proof at room temperature for 20 minutes.

7. Line a baking sheet with parchment. Bake at 355°F (180°C) for 30 minutes. The buns are best eaten fresh but they can be revived with light toasting.

VARIATION

You can also make the sweet version (tanghuoshao) by replacing the spices with ¼ cup (30g) of brown sugar.

RECIPE BY SHELLEY JIANG

Born in Beijing, Shelley loves all things wheat-based, from steamed buns to flatbread to fried dough. As an editor of *The Insider's Guide to Beijing*, *Beijing by Foot*, and *Beijing Eats*, Shelley has scoured Beijing for culinary treats. A trip to France in 2009 inspired her to bake bread from scratch, and she writes about food on her blog. Shelley currently lives in California. www.hawberry.net

AUSTRIAN MIXED GRAIN BREAD

- -

*With its combination of rye, wheat, and spelt flour, and the addition of caraway and fennel seeds,
this loaf is full of aromatic flavors—it will also smell incredible while it bakes.*

INGREDIENTS

1 cup (260 g) wheat sourdough starter
½ cup (50 g) medium rye flour
½ cup (65 g) whole wheat bread flour
1½ cups (150 g) white spelt flour
½ cup (120 ml) water
¾ tsp salt
1 tbsp brown sugar
1 tbsp molasses
1 tbsp vegetable oil
½ tbsp caraway seeds
1 tbsp fennel seeds

METHOD

Day one

1. Measure the sourdough starter into a large bowl
   and return any remaining starter to the refrigerator.
2. Add the rye flour, the whole wheat flour, and
   the water and stir gently to mix (if the mixture
   is particularly stiff add a little extra water). Cover
   with plastic wrap and leave on the counter for
   8 hours or overnight.

Day two

3. Add the remaining ingredients to the refreshed
   starter and mix well. Turn out onto a lightly floured
   surface and knead until smooth (about 10 minutes).
4. Shape into a tight sausage, place in a greased loaf
   pan (or 4 individual loaf pans) and cover with oiled
   plastic wrap. Proof at room temperature for 2½ to
   4 hours, until the dough rises about 1 inch (2.5 cm)
   above the loaf pan(s). Preheat the oven to 425°F
   (220°C).
5. Bake for 10 minutes, then reduce the temperature
   to 400°F (200°C), and bake for a further 30 to
   35 minutes.
6. Remove from the loaf tin(s) and cool on a wire
   rack.

Makes a 1½ lb (675 g) loaf

FLAX PRAIRIE BREAD

When you need to increase your intake of omega-3, this is a good, inexpensive substitute to oily fish.

INGREDIENTS

1 cup (260 g) wheat sourdough starter
2 cups (280 g) white wheat bread flour
¾ cup (180 ml) water
¼ cup (30 g) flax flour
¾ tsp salt
1½ tbsp honey
1½ tbsp vegetable oil
1 tbsp sunflower seeds, to decorate
2 tbsp flax seeds, to decorate
½ tbsp poppy seeds, to decorate

METHOD

Day one

1. Measure the sourdough starter into a large bowl and return any remaining starter to the refrigerator.
2. Add 1 cup (140 g) white flour and the water, and stir gently to mix. Cover with plastic wrap and leave on the counter for 8 hours or overnight.

Day two

3. Add the remaining ingredients to the refreshed starter and mix well. Turn out onto a lightly floured surface and knead until smooth (about 10 minutes).
4. Shape the dough into a tight sausage, gently place in a greased loaf pan, and cover with oiled plastic wrap. Proof at room temperature for 2½ to 4 hours, until the dough rises about 1 inch (2.5 cm) above the loaf pan. Preheat the oven to 425°F (220°C).
5. Spray the loaf with water, scatter over the seeds, and spray again to stick them to the loaf.
6. Bake for 10 minutes, then reduce the temperature to 400°F (200°C) and bake for a further 30 to 35 minutes.
7. Remove from the baking pan and cool on a wire rack.

SOURDOUGH PIZZA BASE

A good base is essential for a great-tasting pizza. Leave plenty of space around the toppings, as the crust will be deliciously chewy and crisp.

INGREDIENTS

½ cup (130 g) wheat sourdough starter

1 cup (140 g) organic stone-ground flour or "00" flour

1 tbsp semolina

½ cup (120 ml) water

1 tsp fine sea salt

1 tbsp extra virgin olive oil

METHOD

1. Combine the sourdough starter, flour, and semolina in a kitchen stand mixer bowl and mix with a dough hook on a low speed for 3 minutes to combine.
2. Slowly add the water until the flour and water are combined (it will be quite a wet dough).
3. Mix the dough for a further 3 minutes on a higher speed, so it becomes more elastic. Cover the bowl with plastic wrap and proof at room temperature for 1 hour.
4. Start the motor running again and add the sea salt. Slowly add the olive oil. Mix on a high speed for a further 2 minutes, until the dough is completely combined.
5. Transfer the dough to an oiled mixing bowl. Cover with plastic wrap and proof at room temperature for 2 to 3 hours. (You can cover the dough with plastic wrap and keep in the refrigerator for the next day, if you prefer a more sour tasting dough.)
6. Divide the mixture in half and roll into balls. Dust the work surface with semolina and flour to give the bread a chewy texture. Roll out the bases with a rolling pin, or stretch by hand for a rustic look.
7. Add tomato sauce, Mozzarella, or your choice of toppings (see below), making sure you leave enough space around the edge of the pizza for the crust to rise. Preheat the oven to 475°F (240°C).
8. Place the pizza on a hot pizza stone or a baking sheet and cook for 7 to 10 minutes, or until the crust is golden and the cheese is gooey.
9. Finish the pizza with a drizzle of extra virgin olive oil and Parmesan shavings.

TOPPING IDEAS:

- Mozzarella, cherry tomato, tomato sauce, garlic and herb oil
- Mushrooms, béchamel, halloumi, and Parmesan
- Goats cheese, caper olives, chilli, caramelized onions, tomato sauce
- Chorizo, goats cheese, roasted bell pepper, tomato sauce, mushrooms
- Sausage, mushroom, Mozzarella, béchamel

RECIPE BY FOXCROFT & GINGER

Foxcroft & Ginger is an artisan cafe-cum-bakery based in London, owned and run by husband and wife duo Georgina and Quintin Foxcroft. F&G specialises in handmade baked goods, cakes, pizzas, and of course all things sourdough. A non-stop 24-hour bakery operation is in place to create their unique sourdough, which is based on a secret family formula and adds a deeper flavor to all of the baked goods. The bread is supplied to a number of top London restaurants, and is also available to purchase in store. www.foxcroftandginger.co.uk

SOUR FLOUR BAGELS

Bagels are made with very stiff dough that is shaped with a hole in the middle, and boiled before being baked. A great bagel will be chewy on the inside, crispy on the outside, and full of flavor. It takes practice to get your perfect bagel, but the results will be delicious along the way.

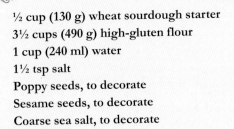

INGREDIENTS

½ cup (130 g) wheat sourdough starter
3½ cups (490 g) high-gluten flour
1 cup (240 ml) water
1½ tsp salt
Poppy seeds, to decorate
Sesame seeds, to decorate
Coarse sea salt, to decorate

METHOD

Stage 1: Make the starter

1. Mix 1 tbsp of starter with ⅓ cup (45 g) flour and ¼ cup (60 ml) water. Let this starter ferment for 6 to 9 hours, until it is bubbly and ripe.

Stage 2: Mixing

2. On a work surface, create a well with the flour large enough to hold the water, starter, and salt. Make sure your flour walls are at least twice as high as the water level, to avoid spilling.

3. Incorporate small amounts of the flour into the water to thicken it, and make sure the starter and salt are evenly spread. As your water becomes less runny, move toward incorporating all of the flour into the mixture. Toward the end of your mix, it will become progressively more difficult.

4. Knead the dough by folding it in half and pressing down, then give a quarter turn and repeat a number of times.

Stage 3: Remixing and fermenting

5. It is possible to get your dough to its completed state after 1 mixing (about 15 minutes), but it is often easier to let the dough relax for 15 to 30 minutes after working it, and then rework it. Between rests, cover your dough with a slightly damp cloth. You are aiming for a completely smooth dough (it can be helpful to flatten by pressing down hard on your dough, trying not to tear it, and then folding it back up). If you do this 2 or 3 times, it makes it easy to get a very strong dough. In your final round, try to end with a rectangular block about 1 inch tall (2.5 cm).

6. After your last working of the dough, cover with oiled plastic wrap and proof at room temperature for 2 to 4 hours to develop the flavor and make it easier to shape.

Stage 4: Cutting and shaping

7. Use a bench scraper to cut the dough in half lengthwise into 2 strips. If your dough was well mixed, you should see a solid inner structure, rather than holes and irregularity. Dip your hands in water, and roll out 1 of the strips. The dough should be slightly wet but not slippery. As you extend your strips lengthwise, their diameter will

shrink. When you've reached a diameter about the size of a quarter, cut your strip into 3 even segments; each of these will be a bagel.

8. Wrap the dough around your hand, overlapping by about 2 inches (5 cm) in the front of your palm. Roll your hand back and forth to seal the bagel. An alternative method of shaping is to cut your entire dough into 6 even pieces and pre-shape into a ball. After a 15 to 30-minute rest, poke a hole through the center of each and pull gently to extend the bagel.

Stage 5: Proofing

9. Place the shaped bagels on a lightly floured board, and cover with a damp cloth to stop them from drying out. Proof at room temperature for about 3 hours, or until they have grown by at least one-quarter. You can now cook the bagels, or place them in the refrigerator and finish the next day.

Stage 6: Boiling and seeding

10. Fill a large pan with 3 inches (7.5 cm) of water.
11. Add 1 tbsp baking soda, which will help to develop the classic texture and taste of the bagel.
12. Bring the water to the boil. Carefully drop each bagel into the water, placing only 2 or 3 bagels per batch, as they will expand in the water. Turn them after about 15 seconds, then remove from the pan after another 15 seconds. If the bagels sink, and stay on the bottom of the pan for more than 5 seconds, they are under-proofed and need more time to ferment. If they become very delicate and collapse, they have over-proofed or did not have a strong enough mix.

13. Dip the bagels into a plate of seeds, or sprinkle seeds or coarse sea salt on top.

Stage 7: Baking

14. Preheat the oven to 480°F (240°C). Place the bagels directly on a baking stone or baking sheet, then slide the sheet into the oven. The bagels will continue to expand until their final crust sets. You can rotate or flip the bagels after 8 to 10 minutes to ensure even baking.
15. Bake for a total of 15 to 20 minutes, and remove as the crust has just turned a deep color. Cool on a wire rack for at least 4 minutes.

RECIPE BY DANNY GABRINER
Founder of Sour Flour, Danny Gabriner started baking in 2009 and soon decided to leave the tech industry to embrace the world of sourdough. Sour Flour is devoted to creating delicious, naturally fermented breads and educating anyone interested in how to bake bread. After just five years, Danny is well known in the San Francisco Bay Area for his high quality sourdough loaves, his aromatic bread and pizza classes, and his generous weekly bagel giveaways (every Monday Sour Flour bakes and gives away hundreds of bagels as a way of connecting with the community).
www.sourflour.org

FLAVORED WHEAT

Adding extra ingredients to your breads adds a depth of flavor and transforms them from the flavor carrier to the main event. All of the breads here use the wheat starter found on page 71, but experiment by adding additional ingredients to your rye breads too.

BAKING WITH EXTRA INGREDIENTS

Bread can include lots of other delicious ingredients like milk, yogurt, eggs, butter, spices, nuts, fruit, and even vegetables. It is important to remember that the only thing yeast really likes is sugar—add sugar to your dough and it will rise more quickly (this is the reason why most factory bread contains sugar).

If you add anything else to bread dough, it will slow down the yeast, and heavy ingredients such as grated carrot, nuts, or fruit will also weigh down the dough. Even light ingredients such as powered spices will slow the rise—as will the addition of eggs, fat, or milk—but that's normal; the yeast simply doesn't like them.

When you add other ingredients to your dough—even dried herbs—it's a good idea to add them after you have kneaded the dough. This is simply because you will destroy the ingredients if you knead them with the dough for ten minutes: fruit will turn into smeary blobs, olives will disintegrate, herbs will become particles, and nuts will hurt your hands. So, knead your dough and put it back in the bowl to rest. After 30 minutes, measure the ingredients, place them on top of the dough and gently fold/squeeze/stretch the dough around the ingredients to ensure they stay intact and are distributed evenly throughout the dough. Don't worry about your dough, as it will recover; worry about the ingredients.

SOAKING DRIED FRUIT

It is a nice idea to soak dried fruit before you add it to your dough. Soaking softens the fruit, and it also means it won't suck all the moisture from the dough as the fruit rehydrates itself. To soak dried fruit, simply cover it with the liquid of your choice and leave it on the counter overnight. You can use water, juice, cold tea or coffee, or alcohol if you wish—red wine, brandy, rum, tequila…they all add a certain something to the dough! The ideal time to soak the fruit is while your starter is refreshing—that way, both will be ready to use the following day. Before you add the fruit, drain it and give it a good shake. Your dough will become slightly wetter for the incorporation of soaked fruit but that's fine—don't be tempted to add more flour.

SOAKING GRAINS AND SEEDS

It's essential that you soak grains and seeds before adding them to your dough. This removes the natural pesticides that the grains and seeds produce, and enables you to digest them better. They will be softer in the mouth so you won't break your teeth, and they will not suck moisture from the dough as they hydrate themselves. To soak grains and seeds you must use liquid that is cold or at room temperature, otherwise you will "cook" the grains and seeds and they will spoil. As with fruit, you can soak these ingredients in any liquid you like. When you drain them, rinse them to wash away the natural pesticides, give them a good shake and add them to the dough. They are pretty robust so you don't have to worry about squashing them; you just need to make sure they are nicely distributed throughout the dough.

DRY-ROASTING NUTS

Dry-roasting nuts before adding them to the dough helps to bring out the oils in the nuts and thus enhances their flavor. Place the nuts in a dry frying pan and stir them constantly over a high heat for 2 to 3 minutes. When they start to turn a golden color and you begin to smell them, remove them from the pan or they will continue to roast—they burn in a second so be careful. Allow them to cool

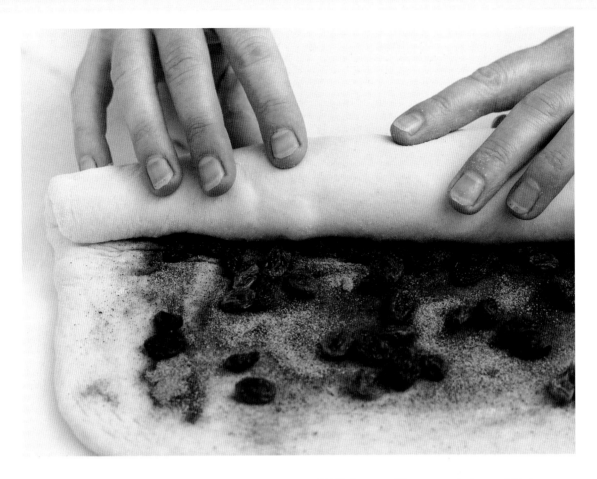

completely before adding them to the dough, or the heat will kill the yeast. You can add them in the same way you add soaked ingredients.

HERBS

You can add fresh or dried herbs to your dough. Knead the dough first then add the herbs as you would anything else, once you have waited for the dough to rest. If you are adding fresh herbs, you may chop them before adding them.

COOKED VEGETABLES

A number of recipes call for sautéed onions in the dough, and for this you need to remember two things. The first is to let the cooked vegetables cool completely before you add them to the dough or they will kill the yeast. You can cook them while the sourdough refreshes and set them aside. Secondly, you should add them once the dough has relaxed, as you do with dried fruit. That way they will maintain their shape and texture to add definitive taste to your bread.

OTHER DELICIOUS THINGS

You can add almost anything to your dough—grated raw carrot, chopped raw onion, different kinds of cheese, olives, pepperoni, sun-dried tomatoes, chili flakes...use your imagination to come up with combinations that sound good to you. As with any ingredient you add, you should knead the dough first and then gently fold in the ingredients.

KNEADING, RISING, AND SHAPING

KNEADING

You can knead dough in a machine but it's better to knead by hand at first to familiarize yourself with the texture of the dough. The better you knead, the better the bread will be. That's because kneading activates the gluten, allowing it to expand and trap the air bubbles that form when the yeast does its work. To knead, you simply stretch the dough over and over again. You can do this in the air, you can pin it down with one hand and stretch it out with the other, or you can fold the dough and slap it down on the surface.

While you knead, you will see the dough change from a ragged mess to a slightly sticky, pillowy ball that you can pick up and stretch so thinly that you can see light through it before it tears (the window-pane test). You should do this with any high-wheat-content dough to check that you have kneaded for long enough (it is impossible with rye dough).

Don't be tempted to add more flour to the recipes—they may be stickier than you are used to but sticky is good. Sticky is also different from wet: some doughs are wet and sticky; others are rather dry and sticky. However, all sourdough doughs are sticky.

It is almost impossible to destroy dough if you are kneading by hand. However, if you are kneading in a machine at too high a speed for too long you can over-knead. If your dough suddenly begins to fall apart and look a bit like spongy cottage cheese floating in a pond, you have over-kneaded it and there is no way to recover; you have to throw it away.

Adding ingredients

If you want to incorporate ingredients like herbs, fruit, nuts, cheese or olives, you should knead the dough then allow it rest a while to soften up, and then add the extra ingredients. Then you put the dough back in the bowl to complete its first rise.

When kneading you stretch the dough over and over again.

Rising (or fermenting or proofing)

You need to let dough rise at various stages that will always be laid out in the individual recipes. Some recipes will instruct you to pop the dough straight in a baking pan once it's kneaded. Other recipes will instruct you to let the dough rise in the mixing bowl, and then complete a final rise in a pan, on a cloth or in a proofing basket (or other container).

There are a few things to remember about the rising process, the main one being that sourdough bread takes much longer to rise than bread made with commercial yeast. Your dough is ready for the oven if it passes the "finger probe test." Simply poke your dough gently but firmly with your finger. If your finger goes straight through the dough really easily, your dough has probably over risen. However, if the indentation springs back completely within a minute, the dough is ready for the oven. This isn't scientific I'm afraid but you will learn from experience.

Rising tips

1. If dough more than doubles in size during its final rise, it may collapse while it bakes. If your dough has clearly collapsed (or climbed straight out of the pan or basket) during the final rise, pull it out, give it a gentle knead with a bit more flour, re-shape it, pop it back in the pan and let it rise again. If you don't realize your dough has over risen, one of the following may happen:
   • It may collapse in the oven.
   • It may spread out like a pancake when you take it out of its form (basket or bowl etc) and put it on the baking sheet.
   • When you cut into the loaf, you may see that the crust has come away from the crumb, leaving a gap between the two.
   • You may see that the top of the loaf is mottled with burned black spots where the crust has come away from the crumb in an irregular way.
2. If your dough has not risen enough in its final rise, it will split in the oven. It usually splits where the dough meets the heat source. In a pan, the split will be along the side of the loaf at the top. If you are baking on a sheet the split will be on the bottom of the loaf or along the side at the bottom.

Shaping

Shaping is the most difficult part of the bread-baking process. Most people were not born knowing how to shape bread, any more than they were born knowing how to play the piano or string a tennis racket. Muscle memory is developed, and with very little practice you will see how easy shaping can be—just be patient with yourself while you learn.

The "science" behind baking is that your dough needs a closed surface structure in order to rise. If the surface of the dough looks like a sponge at a microscopic level, all the gas that the yeast is giving off will escape through the holes and the dough will not rise. If the surface of the dough looks like plastic wrap (no holes at all) all the gas that the yeast is giving off will be trapped and the dough will expand just like a balloon.

Shaping into a basket

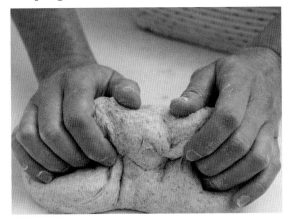 

Stretch and fold the dough into a tight sausage. Seal all the seams and place it seam-side up in the basket. Turn it out of the basket so the seam is down on the baking tray before baking.

Shaping into a pan

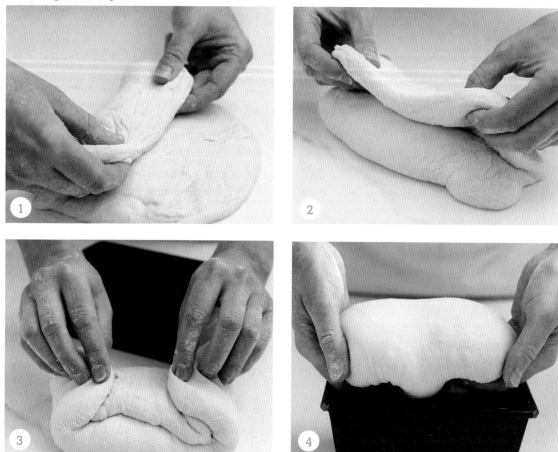

Stretch and fold the dough into a tight sausage. Place it seam-side down in the tin.

It is important to remember this when you're shaping your dough. The aim is to stretch the surface of the dough around itself in a thin membrane that will trap the gas that is given off by the yeast, and expand. When you are shaping sourdough bread remember the yeast is not as powerful as commercial yeast, so you need to be gentle with your sourdough dough. You want to create the surface structure without taking all the air out of it and this is easier said than done. Here are a few points to remember:

- Dry dough is easier to shape. If you are getting frustrated, put a light dusting of flour on your hands and use a scraper to help you move the dough around. Don't flour the table, shaping is much easier if the dough sticks slightly to the surface. That way, when you stretch it, you develop the tension.

- The baking pan is very forgiving when it comes to shaping. If you're uncertain, shape a simple sausage loaf and put it in a pan. The pan will contain your dough and prevent you from getting any unsightly dents in your loaf that may result from imperfect shaping.

- The recipes give you guidance with regard to shaping and there are many other ways to do it. You can watch stretching videos on YouTube!

Braiding dough

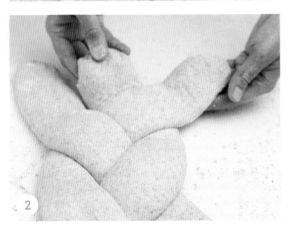

Divide the dough into three equal pieces (use a scale if you do not trust your eye). Braid the dough just like hair. If you are finding it hard, dust the pieces in flour before you braid them.

ONION AND OLIVE BREAD

- -

This delicious bread originates from Greece and Cyprus. Make sure the onion and olive mixture
has cooled completely before adding it to the other ingredients.

INGREDIENTS

1 cup (260 g) wheat sourdough starter
2 cups (280 g) white wheat bread flour
¼ cup (60 ml) water
½ tbsp olive oil
½ onion, finely chopped
½ cup (90 g) black olives, chopped
½ tsp salt

METHOD

Day one

1. Put the sourdough starter in a large bowl and return any remaining starter to the refrigerator.
2. Add 1 cup (140 g) flour and the water and stir gently to mix. Cover with plastic wrap and leave on the counter for 8 hours or overnight.

Day two

3. Heat the oil in a small pan and sauté the onion until just transparent. Add the olives to the onions and set aside to cool.
4. Add the remaining flour and the salt to the refreshed starter and mix well. Turn out onto a floured surface and flatten by hand (or use a rolling pin) into a rectangle about ½-inch (1 cm) thick.
5. Spread the onion and olive mixture over the surface of the dough, leaving a 1-inch (2.5 cm) margin on all sides. Using a paintbrush, brush the edges with water and roll up from the long side into a loaf. Pinch the ends to seal.
6. Place on a floured baking sheet, seam-side down,

cover with oiled plastic wrap and proof at room temperature for 1 hour, or until doubled in size. Preheat the oven to 425°F (220°C).

7. Make several diagonal slashes in the top of the loaf. Bake for 10 minutes, then reduce the temperature to 400°F (200°C), and bake for a further 25 to 30 minutes.
8. Remove from the baking sheet and cool on a wire rack.

5a

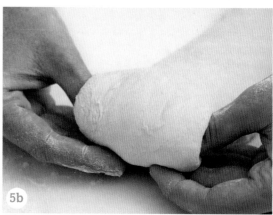

5b

HERB, SPELT, AND WHEAT BREAD

This recipe enables you to compare the leavening characteristics and flavor of spelt with those of wheat flours. It makes a great sandwich loaf.

INGREDIENTS

1 cup (260 g) wheat sourdough starter
2½ cups (250 g) white spelt flour
¼ cup (60 ml) water
⅓ cup (80 ml) milk, plus extra for brushing
1 tbsp melted butter
¾ tsp salt
½ tbsp sugar
½ tsp dried thyme
½ tsp dried oregano
½ tsp dried basil

METHOD

Day one

1. Put the sourdough starter in a large bowl and return any remaining starter to the refrigerator.
2. Add 1 cup (100 g) flour and the water and stir gently to mix. Cover with plastic wrap, and leave on the counter for 8 hours or overnight.

Day two

3. Add the remaining ingredients to the refreshed starter and mix well. Turn out onto a lightly floured surface and knead until smooth (about 10 minutes).
4. Shape the dough into a tight sausage, gently place in a greased loaf pan and cover with oiled plastic wrap. Proof at room temperature for 2½ to 4 hours, until the dough rises about 1 inch (2.5 cm) above the top of the loaf pan. Preheat the oven to 425°F (220°C).
5. Brush the top of the loaf with milk. Bake for 10 minutes then reduce the temperature to 400°F (200°C), and bake for a further 30 to 35 minutes.
6. Remove from the loaf pan and cool on a wire rack.

ROSEMARY BREAD

- -

Fresh rosemary gives this distinctive round loaf a wonderful aroma and flavor, while the raisins add a hint of sweetness.

INGREDIENTS

¼ cup (65 g) wheat sourdough starter

2 cups (280 g) white wheat bread flour

¼ cup (60 ml) water

⅓ cup (80 ml) milk

2 tbsp (30 ml) olive oil

½ tsp salt

½ tbsp sugar

1 tsp chopped fresh rosemary

1 beaten egg, plus extra for glazing

¼ cup (50 g) raisins, plumped (optional, see page 104)

METHOD

Day one

1. Put the sourdough starter in a large bowl and return any remaining starter to the refrigerator.
2. Add 1 cup (140 g) flour and the water and stir gently to mix. Cover with plastic wrap and leave on the counter for 8 hours or overnight.

Day two

3. Add the remaining ingredients (except the raisins) to the refreshed starter and mix well. Turn out onto a floured surface and knead until smooth (about 10 minutes).
4. Gently knead in the raisins (if using) being careful not to break them, as they will be soft. Shape the dough into a tight ball, place it on a floured baking sheet and cover with oiled plastic wrap. Proof at room temperature for 2½ to 4 hours. Preheat the oven to 425°F (220°C).
5. Make a criss-cross slash in the top of the loaf and brush with beaten egg.
6. Bake for 10 minutes, then reduce the temperature to 400°F (200°C) and bake for a further 30 to 35 minutes.
7. Remove from the baking sheet and cool on a wire rack.

Makes a 1½ lb (675 g) loaf

SUNFLOWER BREAD

Sunflower seeds, milk, and honey make this the perfect breakfast loaf. If you prefer a more uniform loaf shape, you could bake this in a pan.

INGREDIENTS

¼ cup (65 g) wheat sourdough starter

1½ cups (210 g) white wheat bread flour

1½ cups (210 g) whole wheat bread flour

¾ cup (180 ml) water

½ cup (70 g) sunflower seeds, plus extra to decorate

½ cup (120 ml) milk

¾ tsp salt

¼ cup (60 ml) honey

METHOD

Day one

1. Put the sourdough starter in a large bowl and return any remaining starter to the refrigerator.
2. Add ½ cup (70 g) white flour, ½ cup (65 g) whole wheat flour and the water and stir gently to mix. Cover with plastic wrap and leave on the counter for 8 hours or overnight.
3. Soak the sunflower seeds in water overnight and rinse well before using.

Day two

4. Add the remaining ingredients, except the sunflower seeds, to the refreshed starter and mix well. Turn out onto a lightly floured surface and knead until smooth (about 10 minutes). Gently fold in the sunflower seeds and make sure they are distributed evenly.
5. Shape the dough into a tight sausage, place it on a floured baking sheet, and cover with oiled plastic wrap. Proof at room temperature for 2½ to 4 hours. Preheat the oven to 425°F (220°C).
6. Spray the loaf with water, sprinkle with the remaining sunflower seeds, then spray again to make sure the seeds stay on. Slash the top of the loaf diagonally.
7. Bake for 10 minutes, then reduce the temperature to 400°F (200°C) and bake for a further 30 to 35 minutes.
8. Remove from the baking sheet and cool on a wire rack.

CHEESE AND ONION BREAD

Adding freshly chopped green onion to cheese bread yields a truly delicious loaf. Toast the slices for a right-out-of-the-oven aroma.

INGREDIENTS

2 cups (520 g) wheat sourdough starter

4¾ cups (665 g) white wheat bread flour

½ cup (120 ml) water

¾ cup (180 ml) milk

2 tbsp sugar

1 tsp salt

2 tbsp melted butter

2 cups (200 g) loosely packed strong
   Cheddar cheese

1 cup (100 g) finely chopped green onion

Beaten egg, to glaze

METHOD

Day one

1. Measure the sourdough starter into a large bowl and return any remaining starter to the refrigerator.

2. Add 2 cups (280 g) flour and the water and stir gently to mix. Cover with plastic wrap and leave on the counter for 8 hours or overnight.

Day two

3. Add the remaining ingredients, except the cheese and onion, to the refreshed starter and mix well. Turn out onto a lightly floured surface and knead until smooth (about 10 minutes). Gently knead in the cheese and onion to distribute them evenly.

4. Divide the dough into 3 even pieces (use a scale or do this by eye). Roll the pieces into long sausages and sprinkle lightly with flour. Braid them into a plait shape and pinch the ends tightly so they don't unravel. Carefully place the braid on a floured baking sheet, and cover with oiled plastic wrap. Proof at room temperature for 2½ to 4 hours.

5. Preheat the oven to 410°F (210°C). Glaze the top of the loaf with beaten egg and bake for 35 minutes.

6. Remove from the baking sheet and cool on wire rack.

ONION LOAF

- -

Onions and rye flour fuse to create a wonderful flavor combination. This recipe uses chopped onions lightly sautéed in olive oil, but raw chopped onions work equally well.

INGREDIENTS

2 cups (520 g) wheat sourdough starter
1 cup (140 g) white wheat bread flour
1 cup (240 ml) water
1 tbsp butter
½ cup (50 g) chopped onions
2 cups (200 g) rye flour
1 tsp salt
1 tbsp olive oil

METHOD

Day one

1. Measure the sourdough starter into a large bowl and return any remaining starter to the refrigerator.
2. Add the white flour and the water and stir gently to mix. Cover with plastic wrap and leave on the counter for 8 hours or overnight.
3. Melt the butter in a frying pan and sauté the onions for 6 to 7 minutes. Transfer to a bowl, cover and set aside until the next day.

Day two

4. Add the remaining ingredients, except the onions, to the refreshed starter and mix well. Turn out onto the counter and knead until smooth (about 10 minutes). Add the onions and gently mix to distribute them evenly without pulping them.
5. Shape the dough into an elongated sausage with pointed ends. Place on a floured baking sheet and cover with oiled plastic wrap. Proof at room temperature for 2½ to 4 hours. Preheat the oven to 425°F (220°C).
6. Slash the top of the loaf in a criss-cross pattern. Bake for 10 minutes, then reduce the temperature to 400°F (200°C), and bake for a further 30 to 35 minutes.
7. Remove from the baking sheet and cool on a wire rack.

BACON, CHEDDAR, AND JALAPEÑO SOURDOUGH

- -

This bread came about from a trip to the farmers' market. The variety of jalapeño I bought was hotter than I was used to but I enjoyed the spice that came with it—if you like the heat, leave the seeds in. This bread makes a great sandwich with extra flavor added from the ingredients in the bread.

INGREDIENTS

For the starter:
1 tbsp wheat sourdough starter
½ cup (70 g) white wheat bread flour
½ cup (120 ml) water

For the dough:
Refreshed starter (minus 1 tbsp)
2 cups (480 ml) water
3 cups (420 g) white wheat bread flour
½ cup (50 g) cubed Cheddar cheese
2 to 3 slices cooked bacon, chopped
2 small or 1 large jalapeño pepper,
    seeded, if liked
1 tsp salt

RECIPE BY DERIK HILL
Derik Hill first became interested in baking when he tried making pizza at home. This led him to other baking experiments and then to sourdough bread. Now he bakes several times a week and is constantly searching for the perfect loaf.
www.houseofbakes.com

METHOD
Day one
1. Put the sourdough starter in a large bowl and return any remaining starter to the refrigerator.
2. Add the flour and water and stir gently to mix. Cover with plastic wrap and leave on the counter for 8 hours or overnight.

Day two
3. Reserve 1 tbsp of the refreshed starter for your next bake. Put the water and refreshed starter in a large bowl to disperse the starter. Add the flour and mix until just combined but not yet smooth. Cover with plastic wrap and proof at room temperature for 1 hour.
4. Add the cheese, bacon, jalapeño, and salt. Mix until well combined and the dough begins to form a smooth ball.
5. Stretch and fold the dough 3 times at 1-hour intervals. Shape into the final loaf, place on a floured baking sheet and cover with oiled plastic wrap. Proof at room temperature for about 1 hour. Preheat the oven to 500°F (250°C).
6. After the final proof put the dough in the oven and immediately reduce the temperature to 450°F (230°C). Bake for 40 to 45 minutes.
7. Remove from the baking sheet and cool on a wire rack for at least 1 hour before slicing.

PLOUGHMAN'S SOURDOUGH

I love food that is multi-functional—in other words not only really tasty, but also healthy and nutritious. This particular sourdough ticks all those boxes. Practically a meal in itself, this loaf is one of my bestsellers at the markets. It's fantastic toasted and eaten with cold meats or a selection of cheese and pickles.

INGREDIENTS

2 cups (520 g) wheat sourdough starter

3 cups (375 g) strong whole wheat bread flour

1 cup (240 ml) dark ale or stout

1 tsp salt

1 sweet apple, skin-on, roughly chopped

2 handfuls walnut pieces

1 tbsp chutney

2 handfuls grated mature Cheddar cheese

RECIPE BY VICKY MANNING

Vicky was never a fussy eater as a child and was an enthusiastic helper in the kitchen. She has always enjoyed making her own bread but only discovered sourdough last year. She started experimenting and in February 2014 decided to try some markets around Glasgow to see if people would be interested in buying her bread. They were and Vicky remains ecstatic. www.thelittlesourdoughbakery.co.uk

METHOD

1. Put the sourdough starter in a large bowl and return any remaining starter to the refrigerator.

2. Add the flour, ale, and salt and mix thoroughly. Once the mixture has started to come together, tip it onto a floured surface and knead thoroughly until you have a stretchy, well-developed dough. It should be springy to touch and not too sticky.

3. Place the dough in an oiled plastic container, cover and proof at room temperature for 6 to 8 hours, until the dough has doubled in size.

4. Tip the dough back onto a floured surface and stretch it into a round, flat shape. Place the remaining ingredients on the dough, and fold it over to cover the ingredients. Knead the dough until all the ingredients are well combined.

5. Divide the dough in half and transfer to floured proofing baskets. Proof, uncovered, at room temperature for 2 to 4 hours. The loaves should have doubled in size when they are ready to cook and feel springy to touch when gently pressed. If your house is particularly warm, it may take less time to proof the loaves so keep an eye on them. Preheat the oven to 425°F (220°C).

6. Once doubled in size, gently tip the loaves onto preheated baking stones and bake for about 20 minutes. Place a tray of hot water in the bottom of your oven to prevent the loaves becoming too hard on the outside.

7. Once baked, the loaves will sound hollow when tapped underneath. Remove from the baking stones and cool on a wire rack.

Flavored Wheat

SWEET BREAD AND BUNS

Sweet breads are a delicious alternative to cakes. They may look incredibly impressive, but the recipes you'll find here use the same basic skills as more simple bread recipes.

SWEET SOURDOUGH BASICS

Sweet bread and buns used to be baked for special occasions—holidays, weddings, and other celebrations. The simple reason for this was that the extra ingredients that make these recipes special used to be very expensive. Eggs, butter, and milk are the usual enriching items that make the crumb soft and the flavor rich. Sugar, spices, dried fruit, and nuts add to the special nature of this category of bread. Today, we can buy most ingredients most of the time, but it's fun to have some delicious, rich bread and bun recipes up your sleeve to bake for a special occasion.

Yeast

Yeast—natural or manufactured—is fussy and it only really likes sugar and water. Ingredients like milk, eggs, butter, spices, fruit, and nuts weigh down the dough and slow down the yeast. Sourdough bread does tend to be a little heavier and chewier than bread baked with yeast, but there are many ways to ensure your sweet bread and buns are light and delicious. You do not have to follow these directions to the letter, as they can be quite fiddly and time consuming, but they will help you achieve lighter, fluffier bread.

Baking basics

Make a pre-dough (also called a pre-ferment or flying ferment).

1. Measure the flour you need for the final dough into a large bowl and make a well in it. Measure the refreshed sourdough (amount stated in the recipe) into the well.
2. Measure the sugar and the liquid into the well, and give the ingredients in the well a good stir.
3. Flick flour over the top of your well to close it and cover the bowl with a tea towel. Let it sit for a couple of hours and you will see that it becomes frothy.
4. Add all the remaining ingredients in the recipes and follow the instructions.

Creating pre-dough increases the yeast activity so when it comes to adding the things the yeast doesn't like, you have maximized the yeast's power.

Add butter last

Flour has an amazing ability to absorb fat, and you want the flour to absorb the butter in its "whole state." Butter is an emulsification, and you don't want it to melt before the flour has absorbed it—once it has melted you can't put it back together again. The heat from your hands can melt the butter, and to avoid this you should knead the dough for a good 10 minutes and then add the butter (cold and cut into small pieces). Then knead again for another 10 minutes or so. The more butter there is, the more messy the job, but don't panic—use a scraper and keep going. The flour will absorb all the butter and your dough will turn a dark yellow color and look and feel a bit like chewing gum.

Heat the milk and cool it down again

When you take milk to boiling point (watch the pan carefully as over-boiled milk is messy) you break down certain enzymes. This not only changes the flavor and the texture of the milk, it also makes the milk less able to hold back the yeast. Just make sure you cool the milk right down before adding it, so you

don't kill the yeast in the sourdough. You can heat the milk, return it to the refrigerator and add it cold to the recipe, if that works better for you. Waiting is boring, and if you are too impatient you might be tempted to add it when it is too hot.

Don't panic at the soft dough

Sweet bread and bun dough tend to be much softer than regular bread dough. At first this can be intimidating, and you might think you have done something wrong. However, it's unlikely you have, so don't be tempted to add any more flour until you have tried a recipe at least a couple of times. You will quickly come to love working with soft dough.

TROUBLESHOOTING
SWEET DOUGH

Problem

Your sweet dough doesn't rise much in the time indicated by the recipe.

Solution

Natural yeast is particularly sensitive to hot and cold, and the difference of just a few degrees in room temperature could change your rising time from 3 hours to 5 or 6 hours. Most of the timings in the recipes reflect the temperature in a warm kitchen, so they are approximate. Sweet dough is ready for the oven when it has risen by one-and-a-half times—sourdough bread rarely rises more than that.

Sweet dough recipes, with their high-enriching ingredients such as butter, eggs, spices, dried fruit, and nuts are even slower to rise than regular sourdough bread. All these ingredients slow down the rising process, so be patient if your kitchen is cool.

Use the finger probe test to check if your bread is ready for the oven. Poke the dough firmly with your finger to make an indentation: if your finger goes straight through, your bread is over-proofed (give it a little knead with more flour, reshape it and let it rise again). If the indentation remains for a minute or more, the bread should proof for a little longer. If the indentation springs back within a minute, it is ready for the oven.

The only place with a constant temperature in most homes is the refrigerator, and you can proof your bread here: simply cover it and put it in the fridge for about 8 hours. It might take a couple of attempts to get the ideal proofing time for your refrigerator (some are a little colder than others, so your dough may take longer than 8 hours to rise).

Problem

Your bread or buns crack at the top, or along the bottom where the dough hits the heat source.

Solution

You have not let the dough rise for long enough. Enriched dough can take hours to rise so be patient – your dough will rise but it may take some time. Butter, milk, eggs, nuts, and fruit all slow down the dough's fermentation. The finger probe test (see page 128) works for sweet bread and buns too.

Problem

Your bread or buns have a mottled top with little burnt spots, and/or the surface has collapsed altogether.

Solution

The dough has risen too much. If you do not catch the dough "on the turn" you will allow it to rise too much, and the dough will collapse in the oven or the crust will come away from the crumb: something you will only see when you cut into it. It can be hard to spot so chalk it up to experience and try again.

Problem

You are having trouble shaping the soft, sticky dough.

Solution

1. Shaping soft dough is tricky but avoid adding more flour to the dough, or flouring the surface, if it's not called for in the recipe. What you can do is have a bowl of flour to hand, and dip your hands in the flour, making your palms and the edges of your hands floury. This will enable you to handle and shape the dough with minimal stick.

2. The first rise of the dough can be done in the refrigerator overnight. The dough will be a little bit tougher due to the cold rise but you will find the dough is super easy to shape. Once shaped, the dough has to warm up before it begins to do its second rise, so anticipate several hours before you can bake the bread.

CINNAMON ROLLS

- -

A delicious, rich loaf that consists of individual raisin-and-spice-filled rolls. These come together during baking but can be gently pulled apart again to eat.

INGREDIENTS

1 cup (260 g) wheat sourdough starter
1½ cups (210 g) white wheat bread flour
½ cup (120 ml) water
¼ cup (60 ml) milk
½ tsp pure vanilla extract
½ tsp salt

For the filling:
1 tsp cinnamon
2 tbsp sugar
1 tbsp melted butter
¼ cup (40 g) raisins, plumped

For the glaze (optional):
1 tbsp melted butter
½ cup (50 g) confectioners' sugar
2 tsp hot milk
¼ tsp pure vanilla extract

METHOD

Day one

1. Measure the sourdough starter into a large bowl and return any remaining starter to the refrigerator.
2. Add 1 cup (140 g) flour and the water and stir gently to mix. Cover with plastic wrap and leave on the counter for 8 hours or overnight.
3. Soak the raisins in water overnight.

Day two

4. Add the remaining ingredients, except the raisins, to the refreshed starter and mix well. Turn out onto a lightly floured surface and knead until smooth (about 10 minutes). Drain the raisins thoroughly.
5. Roll the dough into a rectangle about ½ inch (1 cm) thick. Combine the cinnamon and sugar. Brush the top of the dough with the butter and sprinkle over the sugar-cinnamon mixture, and the raisins.
6. Roll up the rectangle from the long side and slice into 1-inch (2.5 cm) thick slices.
7. Place the slices in a greased round cake pan and cover with oiled plastic wrap. Proof at room temperature for 1 to 2 hours. Preheat the oven to 425°F (220°C).
8. Bake for 10 minutes, then reduce the temperature to 400°F (200°C), and bake for a further 25 to 30 minutes. Remove from the cake pan and cool on a wire rack.
9. While the rolls are still hot, brush the tops with melted butter, or combine the confectioners' sugar, hot milk, and vanilla, and drizzle over the rolls. If the glaze is too stiff to spread, add a little more milk.

>> *See steps on page 132*

CINNAMON ROLLS

- -

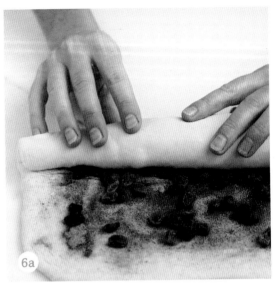

Sprinkle over the sugar-cinnamon mixture and the raisins.

Roll up the rectangle from the long side.

Slice the roll into 1-inch (2.5 cm) thick slices.

Place the slices in a greased round cake pan.

GINGERBREAD

- -

Baking soda helps to leaven this delicious bread so no additional proofing is required.

INGREDIENTS

⅔ cup (175 g) wheat sourdough starter
1 ⅔ cups (230 g) white wheat bread flour
⅔ cup (160 ml) water
2 tbsp melted butter
½ cup (120 ml) molasses
1 tsp ground cinnamon
1 tsp ground ginger
1 egg, beaten
2 tbsp sugar
1 tsp salt
½ tsp baking soda

METHOD

Day one

1. Measure the sourdough starter into a large bowl and return any remaining starter to the refrigerator.
2. Add ⅔ cup (90 g) flour and the water and stir gently to mix. Cover with plastic wrap and leave on the counter for 8 hours or overnight.

Day two

3. Preheat the oven to 400°F (200°C). Add the remaining ingredients to the refreshed starter and mix well.
4. Pour into a greased 8-inch (20 cm) square baking pan.
5. Bake for 55 to 60 minutes.
6. Remove from the baking pan and cool on a wire rack.

>> *See steps on pages 134–135*

GINGERBREAD

3

Add the remaining ingredients to the refreshed starter and mix well.

4

Pour the mixture into a square baking pan.

6

Remove from the baking pan and cool on a wire rack.

CRANBERRY AND NUT LOAF

Choose your own favorite combination of mixed nuts—all varieties taste great in this fruity loaf.

INGREDIENTS

1 cup (260 g) wheat sourdough starter
2½ cups (350 g) white wheat bread flour
1 cup (240 ml) water
¾ tsp salt
1 tbsp sugar
¼ cup (45 g) sweetened dried cranberries
¼ cup (40 g) chopped nuts

METHOD

Day one

1. Measure the sourdough starter into a large bowl and return any remaining starter to the refrigerator.
2. Add 1 cup (140 g) flour and the water and stir gently to mix. Cover with plastic wrap and leave on the counter for 8 hours or overnight.

Day two

3. Add the remaining ingredients, except the cranberries and nuts, to the refreshed starter and mix well. Turn out onto a lightly floured surface and knead until smooth (about 10 minutes).
4. Flatten the dough and scatter the fruit and nuts over the top. Gently knead them in to avoid breaking them.
5. Shape the dough into a tight ball, place in a heavily floured, round proofing basket, and cover with oiled plastic wrap. Proof at room temperature for 2½ to 4 hours. Preheat the oven to 425°F (220°C).
6. Invert the proofing basket and gently roll the dough out onto a floured baking sheet. Slash the top in a star shape.
7. Bake for 10 minutes, then reduce the temperature to 400°F (200°C), and bake for a further 25 to 30 minutes.
8. Remove from the baking sheet and cool on a wire rack.

>> *See steps on pages 140–141*

CRANBERRY AND NUT LOAF

Gently knead the fruit and nuts into the dough to avoid squashing the cranberries.

Flour the proofing basket well.

Place the dough in the proofing basket and cover with oiled plastic wrap or a shower cap.

Proof at room temperature for 2½ to 4 hours and do the finger probe test to check if the dough is ready for the oven.

Makes a 1½ lb loaf

AUSTRIAN CHRISTMAS BREAD

----

*Raisins and candied citron combine with anise to create a festive loaf that is delicious,
and is best served with a generous topping of butter.*

INGREDIENTS

⅓ cup (90 g) wheat sourdough starter

2 ⅓ (325 g) cups white wheat bread flour

½ cup (120 ml) water

¼ cup (60 ml) milk

1 egg, beaten, plus extra to glaze

½ tbsp anise seeds

½ tsp salt

1½ tbsp sugar

¼ cup (40 g) raisins, plumped

¼ cup (50 g) candied citron

METHOD

Day one

1. Measure the sourdough starter into a large bowl and return any remaining starter to the refrigerator.
2. Add 1 cup (140 g) flour and the water and stir gently to mix. Cover with plastic wrap and leave on the counter for 8 hours or overnight.

Day two

3. Add the remaining ingredients, except the raisins and candied citron, to the refreshed starter and mix well. Turn out onto a lightly floured surface and knead until smooth (about 10 minutes).
4. Carefully knead in the raisins and candied citron, then form the dough into a flat oval. Shape into a loaf by folding the top half completely over the dough to meet the bottom edge. Cup your hand over the dough and use the heel of your hand to press down firmly on the edges to seal them.
5. Place the loaf seam-side down on a floured baking sheet and cover with oiled plastic wrap. Proof at room temperature for 2½ to 4 hours. Preheat the oven to 425°F (220°C).
6. Slash the top of the loaf in a diamond pattern and glaze with beaten egg.
7. Bake for 10 minutes, then reduce the temperature to 400°F (200°C), and bake for a further 30 to 35 minutes.
8. Remove from the baking sheet and cool on a wire rack.

>> *See steps on page 140*

AUSTRIAN CHRISTMAS BREAD

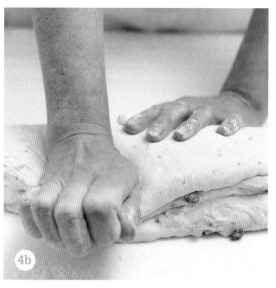

Carefully knead in the raisins and candied citron, then form the dough into a flat oval.

Cup your hand over the dough and use the heel of your hand to flatten and seal the edges.

Slash the top of the loaf in a diamond pattern and glaze with beaten egg.

Remove from the baking sheet and cool on a wire rack.

JASMINE TEA BUNS

- -

These deliciously light buns are the ideal afternoon tea treat. The subtle infusion of jasmine adds an aromatic twist.

INGREDIENTS

For the refreshed starter:
⅓ cup (45 g) white wheat bread flour
2 tbsp almond milk (unsweetened)
1 tbsp wheat sourdough starter

For the dough:
1 tsp Jasmine tea leaves
½ cup (120 ml) hot water (for steeping)
1½ cups (210 g) white wheat bread flour
2 tbsp sugar
2 egg whites
½ tsp salt
2 tbsp unsalted butter

RECIPE BY YUKO IKEDA

Yuko Ikeda was born and grew up in Japan but since moved to the States and currently lives in Santa Monica. She worked her way up the restaurant ladder and is now pastry chef at Hinoki and the Bird in LA. Yuko is obsessed with baking and she blogs about baking and life in Santa Monica. www.akitchenblog.wordpress.com

METHOD

Day one

1. In a mixing bowl, combine the flour, almond milk, and starter. Leave to proof at room temperature for 12 hours.

Day two

2. Steep the tea leaves in the hot water for 3 minutes. Drain the tea, reserving the leaves. Set aside ⅓ cup (80 ml) of jasmine tea, and chop and set aside 1 tbsp of the tea leaves.

3. Add the tea leaves and the remaining ingredients, except the salt and butter, to the refreshed starter, cover with oiled plastic wrap and proof for 30 minutes.

4. Turn out onto a well floured surface, add the salt and knead until the gluten is developed (about 10 minutes).

5. Add the butter and knead the dough again until the gluten is very developed and you can see through the dough when stretched. Place the dough in a bowl, cover with oiled plastic wrap and proof for 2½ to 4 hours.

6. Punch down the dough and put it in the refrigerator overnight.

Day three

7. Remove the dough from the refrigerator and leave at room temperature for 1 hour.
8. Divide the dough into 4 pieces and pre-shape into rolls. Place on a floured baking sheet and set aside to rest for 30 minutes.
9. Shape the dough into buns and set aside for the final rise for 1 to 2 hours. Preheat the oven to 450°F (230°C).
10. Bake the buns for 25 to 30 minutes. Use a garden mister to spray inside the oven to create steam.
11. Transfer to a wire rack to cool.

Kneading tip

The key to soft crumbs and fluffy volume is strong development of the gluten's structure. Knead the dough until it becomes elastic and can be stretched very thinly but is still tough to break. If it's easy to poke and make a hole and the edge of the hole is rough, you need to knead the dough longer and keep checking the consistency of the dough.

CHOCOLATE SOURDOUGH CREAM CHEESE SWIRLS

- -

This breakfast bread is a true delight—soft and cakey with a hint of sweetness. There is just enough chocolate for a treat, but with a lightness that will get your day off to a great start.

INGREDIENTS

For the refreshed starter:
1 cup (260 g) wheat sourdough starter
1 cup (140 g) white wheat bread flour
¼ cup (60 ml) milk

For the dough:
1 tbsp unsalted butter, room temperature
1 egg
2 tbsp sugar
⅔ cup (160 ml) milk
1½ tsp pure vanilla extract
1 tsp (5 g) salt
1 tsp baking soda
½ cup (30 g) cocoa powder
1¾ to 2½ cups (245 g to 350 g) white
   wheat bread flour

For the filling:
1 cup (225 g) cream cheese, softened
¼ cup (25 g) sugar
½ tsp vanilla extract
1 egg
¼ cup (60 g) unsalted butter
⅛ tsp salt

For the icing:
1 cup (110 g) powdered sugar
1 tsp vanilla extract
¼ cup (60 ml) milk

METHOD

1. Put the sourdough starter in a large bowl and return any remaining starter to the refrigerator.
2. Add the flour and milk and stir gently to mix. Cover with plastic wrap and leave on the counter for 4 to 6 hours.
3. In the bowl of a kitchen stand mixer, combine the butter, egg, sugar, milk, vanilla, salt, and baking soda.
4. Carefully mix in the cocoa powder, then add the flour ½ cup (70 g) at a time, to form a soft dough.
5. Switch to the dough hook attachment of your mixer, and knead for about 5 minutes (if the dough is too sticky, add more flour, ¼ cup (35 g) at a time, until it clears the bowl and stays on the dough hook while kneading but is still soft and slightly sticky to the touch).
6. Lightly oil a large mixing bowl, turn the dough into it to coat the top, and cover with oiled plastic wrap. Proof at room temperature for 2 hours, or until doubled in size.

7. Meanwhile, prepare the filling. Using a hand mixer, mix all the ingredients together in a large bowl. Cover with oiled plastic wrap and set aside.

8. Turn the dough out onto a well-floured surface. Roll into a large rectangle, about 12 x 18 inches (30 x 46 cm), using more flour as needed to keep the dough from sticking.

9. Spread the filling evenly over the dough. Roll up the dough from the long side up to form a spiralled log. Cut into 12 even rounds.

10. Place the rounds on a buttered 9 x 13-inch (23 x 33 cm) baking sheet, spaced 1 inch (2.5 cm) apart. Cover with oiled plastic wrap and proof at room temperature for 2 hours, or until doubled in size. Preheat the oven to 350°F (180°C).

11. Bake for 30 minutes. Place the baking sheet on a wire rack to cool.

12. In a medium bowl, mix together the ingredients for the icing until smooth. Drizzle over the swirls and serve. This bread can be stored, loosely covered, for 2 to 3 days.

RECIPE BY JENNIFER WARD AND SHELLEY COONEY

Jennifer Ward and Shelley Cooney became friends while blogging, and they both fell in love with their sourdough starters. They had so much fun finding, developing, and testing fun, new ways to utilize their starters, that they soon found themselves trading recipes back and forth. They decided to start a website and monthly baking group dedicated to sharing their baking adventures with sourdough lovers around the world. www.sourdoughsurprises.blogspot.com

TOP TEN SOURDOUGH TIPS

1. KEEP COOL

You will only kill the yeast if you add anything to the dough that is too hot. To avoid this happening, make sure the water or milk is at room temperature at most—cold is fine, hot is not. Additionally, if you dry-roast nuts, or sauté onions or other vegetables, let them cool completely before you add them to the dough.

2. KNEAD WELL

When working with wheat-family flour, your bread will be better if you knead it well. Whether by hand or machine, knead for a good ten minutes to activate the gluten, and use the windowpane test (see page 143) to check for strength and stretchiness.

3. BUY GOOD-QUALITY FLOUR

Flour is the main event, so buy the best quality flour you can find. By this I mean minimally processed, unbleached and, ideally, with no additives. This can be difficult and you will need to research mills, talk to millers, talk to craft bakers, and experiment with different flours until you find the ones you like. It may be a little more expensive than big brand flour, but it is still relatively cheap. Flour does have a sell-by date, which should be respected, but it's usually pretty long so you can buy in bulk from a miller whose flour you like.

4. FEEL AND TASTE YOUR DOUGH

It is the relationship between how your dough feels and tastes, and how your bread feels and tastes that matters. Some people like salty bread, some like humid bread. Remember what your dough feels like and tastes like (a little raw dough won't hurt you), and then compare that to how the bread feels and tastes when you eat it. Take notes, take photos, and adjust as you become a more experienced baker.

5. BUY AN OVEN THERMOMETER

So many problems can be avoided if your oven is at temperature. Beg, borrow, or buy an oven thermometer and have your oven calibrated by an engineer if need be.

6. ALLOW ENOUGH TIME FOR THE DOUGH TO RISE

The big drag when you are baking is when you have to go out or go to bed, and your dough is not ready for the oven. When you first start, leave plenty of time so you know your dough is ready. On a cold day, dough can take ages to rise and with a little experience you know when this is going to happen. You will also learn when you can pop your dough in the refrigerator to let it finish its rise while you are out (or sleeping). When you are first starting, give yourself a whole day just to be sure. A nice rainy day when going out seems too difficult and a good book seems just right. That is a perfect a day to bake bread for the first time!

7. BE SELECTIVE WHEN YOU BUY EQUIPMENT

If you want to invest in a mixer, buy a good one rather than having to buy and replace mediocre machines. Invest in good pans that don't warp and that don't develop flaky sides and bases. That, however, is about it. Bowls, scrapers, spoons, and measuring equipment do not need to be expensive.

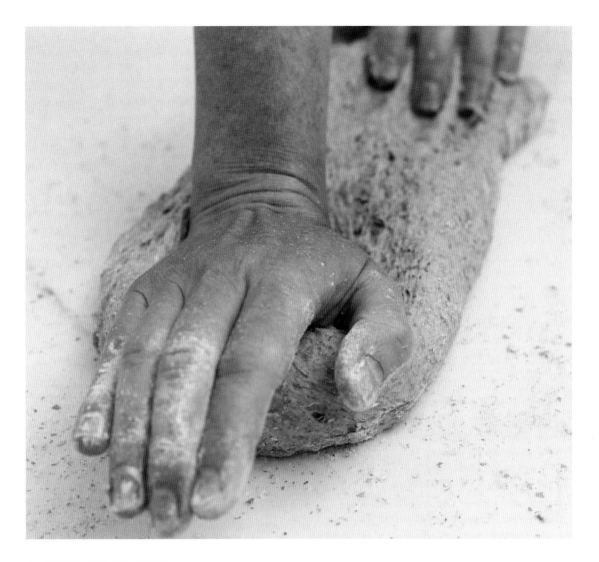

8. KEEP IT SIMPLE

When you are starting out, keep it simple. Simple bread is delicious—dubious combinations of flavors may not be so delicious.

9. HAVE A "GO TO" BREAD

My "go-to" bread is rye. I will mix up enough dough for eight loaves (I have a big oven at home) and I will proof them in the refrigerator overnight. In the morning, I take them out, heat up the oven, and pop them in. When they are cool, I freeze seven of them

and take them out as I need them. The amount of work involved is maybe 30 minutes, and that includes washing up. Perfect!

10. RELAX

The only time the kitchen fairy deserts me is when I am angry or anxious. The thing to remember is the mantra: everything is good toasted, even if it's ugly. It's true.

BREAD AND HEALTH

Grains are basically grass seeds and humans don't eat grass. Eating grass or raw flour would give us an almighty tummy ache, as our tummies would struggle to know what to do and become bloated. Bread, and specifically bread made with wheat flour, has received a lot of bad press over the past few years, with articles about the dangers of consuming grains, and the rise of allergies and intolerances. If you do feel uncomfortable when you eat bread, you should get tested to see if you are a celiac. Celiacs must avoid any food with gluten, which includes bread made with wheat, rye, spelt, emmer, einkorn, kamut, barley, and oats (unless they are labeled gluten free).

Some people who are not celiacs still feel uncomfortable when they eat bread. There could be several reasons for this:

1. Overexposure: a daily diet of highly refined wheat-based breakfast cereal for breakfast, white bread sandwiches for lunch, and pasta for dinner is limited in the extreme. Years of following that diet will put pressure on your system and could make you sensitive to wheat, or particularly, highly refined wheat. Eat everything in moderation is the advice our grannies gave us and they were probably right.

2. Changes in the wheat plant: since the widespread adoption of the combine harvester sometime between the World Wars, wheat that is grown in the west has changed enormously. Not only does it look different, but its molecular structure is also different. Scientists believe that certain people have difficulty digesting modern wheat, as it has changed so much and we haven't. Today, some farmers are returning to what is now called

"heritage wheat." If you find you have a sensitivity to modern wheat, you could try heritage wheat as an alternative.

3. Flour: flour is not clearly labeled everywhere in the world. However, some countries do label flour and you may be surprised to learn that your average bag of flour may not just contain wheat, spelt, or rye. It may, in fact, contain amylase, xylanase, ascorbic acid, niacin, reduced iron, thiamine, mononitrate, L-cysteine hydrochloride, azodicarbonamide, or folic acid. In some countries, additives such as these are listed on the bag of flour. In other countries some of these additives are prohibited or included by law, and in still other countries the additives are not listed. If you are concerned, buy flour direct from a mill and ask what is in it.

4. Bread ingredients: the average loaf of bread shouldn't contain anything other than flour, water, salt, and yeast. If your bread comes in a packet from the supermarket, the ingredients will be clearly displayed but if your bread doesn't come in a packet, they won't necessarily be displayed. Additives in a plain loaf of white or brown bread may include some of those you read about in the section above on flour and, in addition, different kinds of sugar, fats, flour (the addition of soya flour, for example, is common), and additional gluten to help the dough stand up if it is made with weak wheat flour. Read the label if there is one, or talk to the baker if there isn't. And if there isn't a baker to talk to, you may want to reconsider buying the bread just in case.

GLOSSARY

Autolyse
This is the stage where the dough has a rest before being kneaded. It allows the ingredients to mingle before kneading takes place to activate the gluten in the dough.

Baking stone
A flat, heatproof cooking platter that dough is placed on before being baked. They are available in different materials, including granite, iron, stone or ceramic.

Cealiac disease
A condition suffered by about 1% of the population who are highly intolerant to gluten in any form.

Elasticity
The ability of dough to "bounce back." Dough needs the right amount of elasticity to rise properly and keep hold of the gases inside.

Enriched bread
If you add any extra ingredients to your dough—such as chopped nuts, fruit, seeds, or vegetables—the dough is enriched. Added ingredients will have an impact on the proofing time, and the amount the dough rises, as certain ingredients slow down the yeast and others weigh down the dough.

Fermenting/proofing/rising
These are different terms for the step in the baking process when the dough is being filled with carbon dioxide to become lighter, to develop flavor, and to become more digestible. Some recipes call for more than one proof or rise, often with kneading in between to help activate the gluten in the dough.

Final dough
The dough that you will shape and let rise before putting it in the oven to bake.

Gluten
This is a protein created when glutenin and gliadin form a bond. When you knead bread you "activate" the gluten and create a membrane that traps carbon dioxide bubbles as they form, giving volume to the bread. Gluten also gives bread its chewy texture.

Hydration
This is a baking term that refers to how "wet" a dough is. Different types of flour can produce dough that is more or less wet, as they absorb more or less moisture.

Lame

A special razor used to make cuts in dough before it goes in the oven, both to control cracking and to make an attractive pattern.

Levain/poolish/sponge

These are other names for sourdough starters that you are bound to come across if you get the sourdough baking bug.

Peel

A long-handled paddle that is used to remove bread from a baking stone or the bottom of a bread oven.

Pre-dough

A process in some recipes that involve several steps. A pre-dough contains the refreshed starter and some of the ingredients for the final dough. You create a pre-dough to build flavor and develop a certain texture in the bread.

Proofing basket (banneton)

Basket made of cane or pressed wood (or even plastic) in which dough rises for a more rustic and traditional look.

Punch down/de-gas

Recipes sometimes ask you to "punch down" or "de-gas" the dough after the first rise. This helps the gluten relax, gives the yeast fresh air and new food (at a molecular level), and helps the dough rise evenly. It involves pushing back the dough and folding it over a number of times before it rises again.

Refreshed starter

The bubbly, sweet-smelling result of adding fresh flour and water to your sourdough starter. You add the remaining dough ingredients to your refreshed starter to make bread.

Scraper

A small, thin, rectangular paddle with no handle that is invaluable for cutting, kneading, and moving dough.

Sourdough starter

This is the basic paste of flour and water in which the natural yeast is trapped. It takes 4 to 5 days to make and involves gradually adding flour and water to a container. Keep it in the refrigerator in an airtight container, when it has "taken," and take it out when you need to use it.

Spelt, Emmer, Einkorn, Kamut

Varieties of flour that are milled from grains that are distant cousins of wheat. They all contain gluten but have different characteristics to wheat, so the dough and the bread will have a different texture and flavor.

Windowpane test

Once you have kneaded your dough, cut off a small piece and gently stretch it under a light (sunlight or electric). You should be able to stretch it so thinly that you can see light through it. If it tears before you get to that stage, knead it for 2 to 3 minutes more and try again.

RESOURCES

AMAZON

Whichever country you live in, Amazon is an excellent source of baking equipment and ingredients. From pans to proofing baskets, from flour to dried fruit, you can buy almost anything you need to bake sourdough bread from this website. www.amazon.com

KITCHENAID AND KENWOOD

These are both excellent brands of freestanding mixers with dough hooks. Look on their websites for their latest information and prices.
www.kitchenaid.com
www.kenwood.com

BROTFORMEN

This is the best place to find all manner of proofing baskets and other containers for rising bread. The company is based in Germany but will ship orders across the EU and to the USA and Canada. www.brotformen24.de

SOURCING EQUIPMENT

If you type "bakery supplies online" into your internet search engine you will find a great deal of options.

SOURCING FLOUR

If you type "stone-milled flour online" into your internet search engine you will find excellent providers of good-quality, stone-milled, organic and non-organic flour. It is worth doing some research to find the best millers available to you. Shipping flour is not cheap but if you buy it in bulk you will find it is no more expensive than going to the supermarket and carrying it home in small bags.

INDEX

ACKNOWLEDGMENTS

For Harriet who gave me my first sourdough starter and cook book. For all my students who continue to encourage and challenge me. To Lucy and Cara without whom this book would never have been possible.

ABOUT THE AUTHORS

Ed Wood is a sourdough enthusiast, and owner of the successful Ed Wood's International Sourdoughs (www. sourdo.com) based in Idaho, USA. The company prides itself on being a source of authentic sourdough cultures, and ships to countries all over the world. Ed's background includes a PhD from Cornell University with studies in nutrition, and a trip to Egypt with the National Geographic Society to learn how the pyramid builders in Giza made some of man's first leavened sourdough bread to feed 30,000 pyramid builders. Ed is dedicated to testing new cultures, new ingredients, and new ideas to keep the authenticity of sourdough alive. He is the author of *Classic Sourdoughs: A Home Baker's Handbook*.

Jane Mason founded Virtuous Bread (www.virtuousbread.com) in 2010 to make it fun and easy for people all over the world to make, find and learn about bread, and in so doing to forge the link between bread and virtue. Jane bakes, teaches baking, and speaks about bread as a catalyst for social change. Completely self taught, Jane has had the fortune to bake with excellent bakers from South Africa to Sweden, and it is this knowledge of global bread and its role in the lives of billions of people all over the world that makes her special. She is the author of *All You Knead Is Bread* and *The Book of Buns*.

PICTURE CREDITS

p8 Michael Wissing / StockFood, p11 Ina Peters / i-stock, p13 Pål Espen Olsen / i-stock, p15 Victoria Firmston / StockFood, p21 Radu Dumitrescu / Shutterstock, p25 Oliver Brachat / StockFood, p27 B. and E. Dudzinscy / Shutterstock, p39 Oliver Brachat / StockFood, p41 Michael Wissing / StockFood, p99 Wictory / Shutterstock, p143 Valerie Janssen / StockFood, p145 Phleon / Shutterstock.